BELIEVING IN
JESUS CHRIST

Other books in the Foundations of Christian Faith series

BELIEVING IN JESUS CHRIST

Leanne Van Dyk

Foundations of Christian Faith
Published by Geneva Press in Conjunction with
the Office of Theology and Worship, Presbyterian Church (U.S.A.)

Scripture quotations from the New Revised Standard Version of the Bible are copyright © 1989 by the Division of Christian Education of the National Council of the Churches of Christ in the U.S.A., and are used by permission.

Martin Luther King Jr. quotation reprinted by arrangement with the Estate of Martin Luther King Jr., c/o Writers House as agent for the proprietor, New York, NY. Excerpt from *Testament of Hope*, copyright 1968 Martin Luther King Jr., copyright renewed 1996 Coretta Scott King.

Book design by Sharon Adams
Cover design by Night & Day Design

First edition
Published by Geneva Press
Louisville, Kentucky

This book is printed on acid-free paper that meets the American National Standards Institute Z39.48 standard. ∞

PRINTED IN THE UNITED STATES OF AMERICA

02 03 04 05 06 07 08 09 10 11 — 10 9 8 7 6 5 4 3 2 1

Library of Congress Cataloging-in-Publication Data

Van Dyk, Leanne, 1955-
      Believing in Jesus Christ / Leanne Van Dyk.— 1st ed.
          p. cm. — (Foundations of Christian faith)
      ISBN 0-664-50162-1
      1. Jesus Christ—Person and offices. I. Title. II. Series.

BT203 .V36 2002
232'.3—dc21
                                                              2002070581

Contents

Series Foreword

*T*he books in the Foundations of Christian Faith series explore central elements of Christian belief. These books are intended for persons on the edge of faith as well as for those with strong Christian commitment. The writers are women and men of vital faith and keen intellect who know what it means to be an everyday Christian.

Each of the twelve books in the series focuses on a theme central to the Christian faith. The authors hope to encourage you as you grapple with the big, important issues that accompany our faith in God. Thus, Foundations of Christian Faith includes volumes on the Trinity, what it means to be human, worship and sacraments, Jesus Christ, the Bible, the Holy Spirit, the church, life as a Christian, political and social engagement, religious pluralism, creation and new creation, and dealing with suffering.

You may read one or two of the books that deal with issues you find particularly interesting, or you may wish to read them all in order to gain a deeper understanding of your faith. You may read the books by yourself or together with others. In any event, I trust that you will find a fuller awareness of the living God who is made known in Jesus Christ through the present power of the Holy Spirit. Christian faith is not about the mastery of ideas. It is about encountering the living God. It is my confident hope that this series of books will lead you more deeply into that encounter.

Charles Wiley
Office of Theology and Worship
Presbyterian Church (U.S.A.)

Acknowledgments

Writing is, in many ways, a solitary and lonely task. It is in other ways richly communal. I am grateful for the communities of people who contributed to this book. My colleagues at Western Theological Seminary, always a congenial group, encouraged and advised me. The people of the Office of Theology and Worship of the Presbyterian Church (U.S.A.), who sponsored this book and the others in the Foundations of Faith series, were, as usual, wonderful. My gratitude extends most deeply to my husband, Steven Chase, and our daughter, Rachel.

I dedicate this book to my parents, Bill and Elaine Van Dyk. It is from them that I first learned about Jesus.

1

The Very Heart of God: Who Is Jesus?

*Y*ou can order a Visa card from the Internet with a picture of Jesus on it. A Jesus Visa. The Web site pitches this credit card with the line "Show the world your love for the Most High." The idea is, apparently, that the more you use your credit card, the more you can show the world your love for Jesus.

You can load a Jesus screen saver onto your computer. You can buy Jesus playing cards, Jesus bumper stickers, Jesus bookmarks, key chains, lapel pins, and earrings. The idea is, apparently, that these trinkets enhance your relationship with Jesus. Some Christians claim to find comfort and encouragement in them. Others find them an outrageous commercial gimmick.

Jesus is not only used to support the cause of healthy profits and entrepreneurial strategies. Ever since Jesus himself walked and talked with his followers two thousand years ago, people have enlisted him to support a hopelessly long, often contradictory, and sometimes spectacularly foolish list of causes and convictions. Popes, bishops, and soldiers in the Middle Ages understood Jesus as summoning Europe to the cause of the Crusades. Both sides of brutal religious wars have shouted his name. Some have assumed that Jesus approved the colonial conquests of Africa, Asia, South America, and North America in the age of empires. Others have claimed that he allowed, even required, the institution of American slavery.

In contemporary America, racists have used the name of Jesus to defend discrimination, sexists have excused the marginalization of women, and the rich have justified their wealth. The name of Jesus is used by candidates for political office to win votes. It is used by television evangelists to raise money. For some, the name of Jesus is a curse word, for others, a sort of verbal mortar to shore up an impoverished vocabulary.

The name of Jesus is also the source and motivation of countless acts of generosity, kindness, and compassion. People have founded hospitals in the name of Jesus. They have built houses for needy families with volunteer hours and donated goods in the name of Jesus. They have tirelessly advocated for justice and struggled for righteousness. They have adopted special-needs children and run honest businesses, all in the name of Jesus. They have chopped onions in soup kitchens and organized political action for better training programs for welfare mothers. This, too, has been done in the name of Jesus.

Even a brief survey of this long list, by turns either sordid or splendid, raises urgent questions: Who is Jesus? What did he do for us? How is human life different because of Jesus? What can we hope for in the future? These questions have been asked by Christians and non-Christians for many hundreds of years. They will emerge repeatedly in the pages of this book.

Jesus Is the Christ

Jesus once said to his disciples, "Who do people say that I am?" His disciples began listing off some of the things they had heard. "Some folks think you are John the Baptist, come back from the dead." "Well, I heard someone say you are Elijah or Jeremiah." "I heard that too—or that you are another prophet." Jesus listened to all this and then asked, "But who do you say that I am?" The impulsive and enthusiastic Peter quickly replied, "You are the Christ, the Son of the living God!" (Matt. 16:16).

This confession of faith in Jesus as the Christ is at the very center of the Christian faith. From the beginnings of the Christian community in the days of the missionary apostles to the worldwide church today, Christians confess Jesus as Lord and Christ. In the first few decades of the Christian community, the words "Jesus is Lord" were a compact summary of what it meant to be a Christian. It became a small creed, a short declaration that captured everything most crucial to the faith. When Paul wrote a letter to the church in Philippi, he quoted an early Christian hymn that contains this small creed,

> Jesus Christ is Lord,
> to the glory of God the Father.
> (Phil. 2:11b)

But what that confession really means has varied enormously over the twenty centuries of Christian belief. One person might say, "It means that Jesus is my personal Lord and Savior and, if I believe in him, I will have eternal life." Someone else might say, "It means that Jesus is on the side of the poor and oppressed and we are called to join in the struggle for justice." Yet another person might declare, "Jesus is King of the world. We must follow Jesus and obey him." Someone else might answer, "Yes, Jesus is King. But his rule is best seen in the suffering of the cross. We must turn upside down all our notions of power because of Jesus."

Even those who knew Jesus, who listened to him, followed him, and sensed his remarkable presence, were divided on his true identity. It is perhaps not surprising, then, that divisions and disagreements have always swirled around Jesus. Some people have concluded that Jesus was a social reformer who failed; others have claimed he was a person with extraordinary religious and spiritual sensitivities; still others have insisted he was a political agitator; yet others say he was a man uniquely chosen by God to spread the message of love and justice. Some have pictured him as meek and mild; others, as a conquering warrior. Some sincere Christian people insist on the necessity of certain carefully chosen words to identify Jesus, words often laden with rich tradition. Others vigorously propose new words, new concepts, new ideas about Jesus.

In the novel *The Brothers K,* author David James Duncan tells the story of the Chance family, a family of four boys, two girls, an agnostic father, and a mother of passionate fundamentalist faith.

One of the themes of the novel is an exploration of the question "Who is Jesus?" Each of the children must learn to navigate the treacherous waters of their parents' feuds about God, the Bible, and Jesus. Each child attempts to find some sense in it all.

One of the boys, Kincaid, sums it up this way:

> It's strange the way everybody has their own pet notion about Jesus, and nobody's pet notion seems to agree with anybody else's. Grandawma, for instance, says He's 'just a defunct social reformer.' Then there's Papa, who once said he's God's Son all right, and that He survived the crucifixion just fine, but that the two-thousand-year-old funeral service his cockeyed followers call Christianity probably made Him sorry He did. Meanwhile there's Freddie, who's six now, and who told me she saw Christ hiding under her bed one night. . . . And Bet, who spent a whole day making a Christmas card for Uncle Marv and Aunt Mary Jane last year, then got so proud of the card that she refused to mail it to anybody but herself. . . . Then we looked to see what she was proud of, and it turned out to be this whole army of crayon angels, in these gold sort of football helmets, charging into Bethlehem while in the sky above them huge red and green letters copied from a Christmas carol book Bet couldn't yet read proclaimed: "JOY TO THE WORDL! THE SAVIOR RESIGNS!"[1]

Kincaid is right—there have been a lot of notions about Jesus, and many of those notions do seem to collide with one another. Sometimes, fears and suspicions mount on both sides. Armies have clashed over competing accounts of the Christian faith. Churches have split over how to put into words the identity of Jesus Christ and how the saving life, death, and resurrection of Jesus Christ can best be understood. The history of the Christian church has been marred again and again by conflict and division over precisely the confession that should have united it: the confession of Jesus as the Christ.

In spite of all the sad and sorry divisions, there has also been remarkable unanimity among generations of believers. For two thousand years, Christians have worshiped Jesus Christ, com-

---

[1] David James Duncan, *The Brothers K* (New York: Bantam Books, 1996), 61.

muned with him in the Lord's Supper, and engaged in acts of justice and mercy in his name. Even though Christian believers of different times, different languages, and different cultures all express their faith in Jesus Christ in a wondrous diversity of ways, all can come together in a common commitment to Jesus. The broad and deep Christian tradition affirms that in Jesus Christ, the very heart of God is displayed. All Christians further recognize that Jesus lived a life of perfect obedience and communion with God. Believers agree that Jesus died for the sins of the world, sent the Holy Spirit to gather us together into a community of love and worship, and promised to come again to bring us at last to our true home, a home of shalom with God and one another.

How *exactly* and why *exactly* Jesus displays the heart of God is a mystery of daunting depth. Somehow, God's mercy for human beings is made visible in Jesus. Somehow, Jesus displays to us the true God, the God of mercy, love, compassion, and forgiveness. Somehow, the love of God includes as well the judgment of God. Somehow, the death and resurrection of Jesus proclaims a loud "No" against everything that conspires to destroy the good gifts of God. Somehow, God will accomplish the goal of restoring peace and joy to the world, wiping away all tears and healing all wounds. Somehow. It may be that we will someday understand all the details of God's reconciling the world to God's self in Jesus Christ. Perhaps we will have the opportunity to ask God what puzzles and confounds us about the ways of God with the world. It may also be that all our doubts and questions will melt away in the new heaven and the new earth as we join in the chorus of angels and archangels, with all the saints, singing praises to Jesus, "in [whom] all things hold together" (Col. 1:17).

The Lord's Supper liturgy of many Christian churches includes three short sentences: "Christ has died. Christ is risen. Christ will come again." These simple statements summarize the faith of the ages, the faith of our fathers and mothers in past generations, the faith that has sustained people in suffering, the faith that supports people with hope. It is the faith that, although expressed in three succinct sentences in the Communion liturgy, has unfolded in a rich, often dramatic story since the birth of the Christian church.

The Beginning of the Story

The most important sources for learning about Jesus are the four Gospels in the New Testament. Matthew, Mark, Luke, and John each tells the story of Jesus, each from his own particular point of view. Although a couple of other ancient documents, which are not contained in the New Testament, give accounts of Jesus as well, it is the four Gospels that give us the most information about him.

Luke begins his story of the birth of Jesus with an imperial decree. "In those days a decree went out from Emperor Augustus that all the world should be registered" (Luke 2:1). It is unlikely that the whole *world* was registered. Most likely, people in the territory ruled by King Herod were to be counted so that taxation rates could be calculated. The census was for the purpose of raising revenue. One of the requirements of the census was that each man must return to the town of his birth, there to be registered. This rather cumbersome method of a census count proved a heavy burden for one young woman, named Mary. She accompanied Joseph, the man she was to marry, who was required to present himself in person in Bethlehem, the town of his ancestors. Nine months pregnant, she was obliged to walk the distance of more than fifty miles from Nazareth, in the northern region of Galilee, to Bethlehem, just south of Jerusalem. The road was often steep and narrow, and probably crowded with other walkers traveling for the same reason she and Joseph were.

There were, perhaps, other pregnant women who had to walk long, hard miles as well. But this particular young woman was about to give birth to a most extraordinary baby. And Mary knew it. She had been informed by an angel some months earlier that she was to give birth to the Messiah, the Savior, and was to name him Jesus.

Luke reports the angel's visit to Mary in a straightforward way. The angel greeted Mary politely. Mary, naturally, was alarmed at this sudden visitor. Sensing her anxiety, the angel first reassured her and then presented God's plan to her, one that depended in good measure on her. "You will conceive in your womb and bear a son, and you will name him Jesus. He will be great, and will be called the Son of the Most High, and the Lord God will give to him the throne of his ancestor David. He will reign over the house of Jacob forever, and of his kingdom there will be no end" (Luke 1:31–33).

At this point, Mary asked for a clarification: "How can this be, since I am a virgin?" At the angel's reply, Mary must have felt her life shift, like a door on a hinge. Nothing would ever be the same after the angel's answer. The angel said, "The Holy Spirit will come upon you, and the power of the Most High will overshadow you; therefore the child to be born will be holy; he will be called Son of God" (Luke 1:35). Mary's first reaction to this stunning announcement—a child, named Jesus, who will be called the Son of the Most High—is not recorded for us in Luke. The Gospel text reports her calm agreement to the plan: "Here am I, the servant of the Lord; let it be with me according to your word" (Luke 1:38).

Neither does Luke tell us about Joseph's reaction to this news. Certainly, the fact that God had chosen Mary impacted his life as well. Matthew's Gospel account does report on Joseph's initial bewilderment. In an effort to avoid the whole messy scenario, he seriously considered breaking the engagement with Mary. But an angel visited Joseph as well, in a dream, and the question of his support for Mary was never again raised in the biblical story. Only the smallest hints in the Gospels are given of Joseph's role as Jesus' earthly father. But the hints that are given here and there seem to indicate that Joseph was an attentive and caring father, raising the firstborn son, Jesus, along with the rest of the children born to Mary and Joseph.

Every baby's birth, of course, is a miraculous event. Breathless fathers have always called grandparents and aunts and uncles and friends with the news. A beautiful baby. The mother tired, but happy. The labor pretty tough, but everyone is fine, just fine. Jesus' birth, too, was miraculous in this ordinary way. The circumstances were somewhat unusual, it is true. Born in a farmer's animal shelter, perhaps a cave, he was wrapped in the customary strips of cloth that Mary had brought with her for this purpose. She laid him in a manger, a feeding trough for the animals, because the local inn was fully booked. But in every other respect, the birth joined uncounted others before and after in its ordinariness.

The birth announcement was another matter. An angel suddenly appeared to a small cluster of shepherds tending their flock of sheep in the fields outside of town. Traditionally, the shepherds have been imagined as middle-aged, bearded men. It may be, however, that they were young women or even children. Often the chore of watching the sheep fell to the youngest members of the household. The Old Testament book of 1 Samuel tells the story of the child David, the future king of Israel. Too young to go to war with his older brothers, he had the task of family shepherd. In Israel today, as well as in other cultures, typically it is the children who are the sheep herders and tenders.

Why the angel was sent to announce the birth of the Savior to a small group of sheepherders is one of the more puzzling features of this remarkable story. Why not all the people in the over-crowded town inn? Why not the priest at the local synagogue? Why not the mayor of Bethlehem? Surely, these people would have had much more power and influence in society than a bunch of shepherds. Yet, it is not unlike God to reveal God's self to the poor and lowly, the weak and small. Jesus himself, during his ministry thirty years later, repeatedly associated himself with the lowliest and most overlooked members of society. Sending the angel to announce Jesus' birth to a scared group of shepherds sounds just like something God would do.

A great chorus of angels then appeared before the shepherds and sang,

> "Glory to God in the highest heaven,
>   and on earth peace among those whom he favors!"
>   (Luke 2:14)

It was as if the boundaries of heaven itself could not contain the joy and celebration of the heavenly community. Heaven spilled out onto the field of sheep.

The shepherds ran—not out of fear and panic, but with excitement and joy fueling their mad dash to town. Somehow, they found the place where Mary and Joseph and the infant, Jesus, were resting. Somehow, they managed to blurt out the story. Somehow, the word spread around town. Instead of dismissing the shepherds as crazy, the townspeople apparently believed them. "All who heard it were amazed at what the shepherds told them" (Luke 2:18). Mary, characteristically, took everything in and thought it through. Luke tells us that "Mary treasured all these words and pondered them in her heart" (Luke 2:19).

Some artists and painters have attempted to capture this quality of Mary. On my office wall is a poster of a Rembrandt painting. Titled *The Holy Family,* the picture shows Mary standing beside a wicker cradle, rocking it with one hand. In the other hand is a book, open to the page she is reading. The painting speaks of both the tender quality of Mary and her reflective, thoughtful quality. It also speaks of her receptivity to the word of God, symbolized by the book as well as the infant Jesus in the cradle. Sometimes the portrayal of Mary with an open book, depicted by many artists, is called "the Scholar Madonna." It is unlikely, of course, that Mary actually was a scholar. Young Jewish girls at that time did not have access to an education. But the scholar-Mary motif expresses the small hints the Bible gives about the wisdom and thoughtfulness of Mary.

The Gospel of Matthew includes some dramatic and tragic events that occurred shortly after the birth of Jesus that Luke and the other Gospel writers do not mention. Sometime later, perhaps a year or two, wise men came from the East, inquiring about a royal birth that had been indicated in their observations of the stars. They went straight to the palace to ask King Herod. Jealousy and paranoia immediately provoked Herod to suspect a plot to overthrow him. These foreigners were asking about the king of the Jews? *He* was the king of the Jews! This usurper must be destroyed!

So Herod made a callous and cruel decree. All the children under the age of two in and around Bethlehem were to be killed. The murderous order was carried out, and mournful wailing filled the streets and houses of the town. Matthew quotes a poignant verse from the prophet Jeremiah to describe the tragedy:

> A voice is heard in Ramah,
>   lamentation and bitter weeping,
> Rachel is weeping for her children;
>   she refuses to be comforted for her children,
>   because they are no more.
>
> (Jer. 31:15)

Parents weeping for their murdered children in the dark and despair of the night is an image of unbearable grief and intensity. It is a story not limited to that terrible night. All parents who have lost children to violence and injustice join their voices of wailing and loud lamentation to the grieving parents in Bethlehem that terrible night.

Yet Jesus and his parents escaped unharmed. An angel—yet another angel!—had warned Joseph in a dream about the impending disaster. Not waiting a moment, Joseph, Mary, and Jesus fled to Egypt. They knew the long arm of Herod could find them anywhere in Israel. They had to become refugees in a foreign country until the danger passed. When King Herod died, an angel made one more appearance to Joseph, a third time, again in a dream. The angel sounded the "all clear," and the refugee family returned to Nazareth, the town where Jesus grew up. The story of Jesus' childhood is not told by any of the Gospel writers. Luke only reports that "the child grew and became strong, filled with wisdom; and the favor of God was upon him" (Luke 2:40). It is not too much to assume that Jesus played with his friends and his siblings, helped his father in the carpentry shop, and learned to read in the local synagogue school.

People sometimes wonder if Jesus knew he was the Messiah, the Holy One, the Son of God, all the things that the angel told Mary. The nature of Jesus' own self-consciousness or self-awareness is impossible to know completely. Certainly, when Jesus was a newborn baby, not yet able to focus his eyes on anything and only conscious of discomfort and comfort, he did not know he was the Son of God, the Christ. When he was beginning to walk on wobbly legs, he did not know he was the Son of God, the Christ. When he was learning to talk and say his alphabet, he did not know he was the Son of God, the Christ.

But at age twelve, perhaps he had some growing awareness of his identity. He and his family had gone up to Jerusalem for the Passover festival. When it was time to leave and walk back home to Nazareth, Mary and Joseph assumed he was with his friends and started out. That evening, when Jesus did not appear, the worried parents hurried back to Jerusalem and began a frantic search. Finally, Jesus was found in the Temple, sitting with the wise scholars and teachers, listening, asking questions, and amazing the learned elders with his understanding and wisdom. When his parents found him, they blurted out, "Why have you done this? We have been so worried!" Jesus responded, "Why were you searching for me? Did you not know that I must be in my Father's house?"

This story, recorded only in Luke, gives a hint of Jesus' early awareness of what the angel had declared to Mary before his birth. Throughout his adolescence and early adulthood, Jesus gradually understood more and more that he had a unique identity and was sent by his heavenly Father for a unique work.

The Years of Ministry

One morning, when Jesus was a grown man about thirty years old, he was walking by the Sea of Galilee. He spotted two men fishing from a boat just off the shore. Jesus called out to them, "Follow me, and I will make you fish for people!" As if that shouted command were not remarkable enough, these two men immediately abandoned their fishing nets, their boat, their livelihood and daily routine, and followed Jesus.

The four Gospel writers, Matthew, Mark, Luke, and John, all tell stories about the years of Jesus' public ministry with his chosen disciples and numerous other followers and friends. These stories offer us glimpses into the daily life of Jesus, the way he interacted with people, the way he talked. Only his disciples, friends, and family had the benefit of knowing the tone of his voice, his habits, his unique personality quirks, and his laugh. But the Gospel stories give us a fascinating and rich picture of Jesus during these years of teaching, healing, and proclaiming the kingdom of God. Sometimes we can even imagine ourselves in the stories, perhaps standing at the sidelines, watching carefully the way of Jesus with people, observing people's responses to him.

The Gospel of John admits quite frankly that many things had to be omitted in telling the story of Jesus. The very last sentence of John says, "But there are also many other things that Jesus did; if every one of them were written down, I suppose that the world itself could not contain the books that would be written" (John 21:25). The Gospels concentrate on what is truly important. Mark begins his Gospel with the announcement, "The beginning of the good news of Jesus Christ, the Son of God." Mark makes clear from the first words that this is not a story of just any miracle worker. This is not a story of just any itinerant teacher and sage. This is the story of Jesus Christ, the Son of God. This is the Good News.

The Gospels do not include the wealth of details and personal anecdotes of a standard biography today. Yet, we do begin to recognize the character of Jesus as portrayed in the four Gospels. We see Jesus healing people with illnesses both physical and mental. Jesus heals ten men with leprosy (Luke 17), a blind man (John 9), and people possessed by demons (Mark 1). Jesus notices and respects people who are scorned by society. Jesus actually sits down and has a conversation with the Samaritan woman in John 4, much to his disciples' dismay. After all, Jews and Samaritans had some long-held grudges against each other; any social interaction was strictly discouraged. Jesus pays attention to children and tells his disciples not to dampen their spirits and prevent them from coming to him (Mark 10). Jesus even refuses to condemn people who were clearly breaking religious law. He allows his disciples to pick grain on the Sabbath (Mark 2), and he quietly defuses a crowd's bloodthirsty impulse to stone a woman caught in adultery (John 8).

For three years, Jesus was an itinerant teacher and healer. His activities focused mostly in his own province in the northern regions of Israel, in Galilee. The Gospels occasionally tell stories of Jesus' teachings and miracles to the large crowds of people that followed him. His Sermon on the Mount, which Matthew records, was addressed to a large crowd. His feeding of the thousands of men, women, and children was an event of enormous proportions, from a boy's simple lunch of bread and fish. Jesus gave thanks to God, divided the lunch, and the whole crowd was fed. To bring home the point of God's bounty and generosity, the story in Mark 6 makes the additional point that twelve baskets of leftovers were gathered up after all had eaten.

But, for the most part, the Gospels focus on Jesus' interactions with small groups of people or individual people. The disciples, frequently bumbling and fearful. The women friends, portrayed as loyal and strong. Nicodemus, filled with longings and questions. Jairus, the synagogue ruler sick with grief over a daughter who died. Mary and Martha and Lazarus, dear friends. The children. Zacchaeus. Assorted tax collectors and prostitutes. Blind people. Lame people. Crazy people. The Gospel portraits of Jesus are sketched and filled in with these small encounters. What emerges is a portrait of a Jesus with compassion and determination, as well as a keen eye for hypocrisy, a passion for justice, and a willingness to take seriously every person who sought him out or wandered into his path.

If this were all there was to Jesus—an outstanding human being brimming with generosity and wisdom—it might be a story worth telling. Goodness knows, there are all too few such people in the world. But there is more. Far more is claimed about Jesus than his admirable social consciousness and the wit of his parables. The Christian faith confesses that this Jesus is the Christ, the Son of the living God, the Savior of the world, the hope of the nations.

The Trial and Execution of Jesus

An international student of theology, not entirely familiar with English expressions and idioms, once asked me, "Why do you call it *'Good* Friday'?" He was puzzled why the church's somber commemoration of Jesus' crucifixion was called "good." I asked him what was the English equivalent for Good Friday in his language. He thought for a moment and said, "It's something like *Great* Friday." He explained that the meaning was that this day was momentous, significant, weighty. But not good.

Good Friday is good only in the sense that God, in eternal love and mercy, determined to reconcile the world, alienated and separated from God by sin, through the death and resurrection of Jesus. The events of Jesus' arrest, torture, trial, and execution told by all four of the Gospel writers certainly do not read as a good story. The descriptions in the Gospels of the beatings and tauntings of Jesus are excruciating. The trial was clearly a blatant miscarriage of justice. The crucifixion itself was cruel to the extreme, death occurring as a result of prolonged exposure, suffocation, and pain. On the face of it, it is nothing short of outrageous that the Christian faith focuses on the cross as the source of salvation.

The apostle Paul knew this. Writing to the growing Christian churches several decades later, he knew that the cross was a stumbling block to people, that it was foolishness. He knew that people would recoil in horror from the declaration that our salvation comes through Jesus' death. Yet, he also knew that, in God's good plan, the cross was a vital link in the way of reconciliation. He said to the Christians in Corinth, "I decided to know nothing among you except Jesus Christ, and him crucified" (1 Cor. 2:2). Paul declared, knowing how crazy it sounded, that the death of Jesus on a Roman cross is a decisive event of the love and mercy of God.

In recent years, some people have vigorously denied that there is anything "good" about the cross of Jesus Christ. They have rejected any traditional Christian confession of the cross as bringing salvation to humanity. For these people, the cross is an outrage, pure and simple. It is a tragedy, a crime, an instance of undiluted human insanity. From one point of view, the cross is a crime. The quick capital sentence pronounced on Jesus, a sentence based on rigged evidence, does not pass even a minimal standard of judicial procedure. Commenting on the crucifixion, one theologian said, "The whole episode, from a human point of view, was a banal, if brutal, act of judicial murder to preserve the structures of security and privilege which the powerful of this world call 'peace.'"[2]

---

[2] Brian V. Johnstone, "Transformation Ethics," in *The Resurrection,* ed. Stephen Davis, Daniel Kendall, and Gerald O'Collins (Oxford: Oxford University Press, 1997), 348.

But the observation that the cross is a crime is based only on the court record. There is another perspective on the cross of Jesus. It is the perspective of faith. For more than twenty centuries, Christians have believed that the awful story of Jesus' death is, in fact, the story of God's decisive love for the world. In the life, death, and resurrection of Jesus, we see the gracious and forgiving heart of God. The cross reveals not a tyrant God, but a God of love. The death of Christ is precisely how we are made alive in God.

The perspective of faith does not dissolve the scandal or the foolishness of the cross. But it should give Christians the confidence to join Paul in claiming that, even though the cross looks like nonsense to the world, nevertheless the crucified Jesus is the wisdom of God (1 Cor. 1:18). The mystery of the cross remains acute for believers. Christians should not be surprised that some people utterly reject the cross and its message of healing and reconciliation for all. Yet, believers take their comfort and hope in the cross, knowing that a logical explanation of how salvation comes through the death of Jesus Christ is not necessary. Following Jesus is what is expected of Christians. Not explaining Jesus.

The events of the trial and death of Jesus are told in graphic detail in all four Gospels. Far more space is given to the events of those last days, hours, even minutes, than all the previous years combined. The life of Jesus is treated quickly. Some of the healings are recorded. Some of the parables are told. Some of the contours of Jesus' life with his disciples and friends begins to emerge. But we don't know how many brothers and sisters Jesus had. We don't know how he was educated. We don't know how he related as an adult to Mary and Joseph. The Gospel writers are most interested in recording the events of Jesus' death and then his resurrection. These, clearly, are the events that really count.

The political authorities, the officials of the Roman occupation, were increasingly suspicious of Jesus as a potential insurgent. They heard him declare that the kingdom of God was imminent. Such a claim, in their ears, could only mean a scheme against their own authority. Jesus' own disciples hoped that he intended to lead a coup d'état against Rome. In addition, the religious authorities began to resent Jesus. The Pharisees and the Saducees particularly, two influential Jewish parties, saw Jesus as a threat to their own power and prestige. A tide of resentment and anger against Jesus began to rise, with increasing intensity and complexity. At the time of Jesus' arrest, the forces against him, both political and religious, had lost any semblance of good process and judicious order. Eventually, a potent blend of mob frenzy and shrewd political calculation combined to condemn Jesus to death.

Did Jesus know what was going to happen? Did he know the full meaning of what was building up around him? The Gospels indicate that Jesus did know his identity as the Messiah. Jesus was aware of the collision course he was on with the political and religious authorities. Mark 8:31–32 reports that Jesus "began to teach them that the Son of Man must undergo great suffering, and be rejected by the elders, the chief priests, and the scribes, and be killed, and after three days rise again. He said all this quite openly." In the next chapter, Jesus tried to explain to his disciples exactly what was going to happen. He said, "The Son of Man is to be betrayed into human hands, and they will kill him, and three days after being killed, he will rise again" (Mark 9:31).

John's Gospel, too, indicates Jesus' growing awareness of his identity as God's own Son and his call to fulfill the task of the Messiah. John's Gospel is famous for portraying the remarkable relationship between Jesus and his heavenly Father. At one point in John's narrative, Jesus struggles with dread and fear of his impending death. He prays, "Now my soul is troubled. And what should I say—'Father, save me from this hour'? No, it is for this reason that I have come to this hour. Father, glorify your name" (John 12:27–28). For only the second time in the Gospel accounts, God answers Jesus in a voice from heaven. God reassures Jesus by saying, "I have glorified it, and I will glorify it again" (John 12:28). Some of the people standing around heard this voice. Others thought it was thunder, and yet others thought the sound was an angel's voice.

The pace of the story in the Gospels begins to slow down even more with the account of the Last Supper. More details are included. More conversations. More careful attention to what happened, when, and where. All four Gospel writers were concerned to tell this part of the story with special care. We are told small bits of information that bring us into the story. We can picture Jesus and his disciples finishing their Last Supper and singing a hymn together. We can see them walking across the Kidron Valley and entering a small garden named Gethsemane, a particular favorite of Jesus for meeting with his disciples and for prayer to his Father in heaven.

In the Garden of Gethsemane, the distress and anxiety of Jesus became acute. Mark tells us that he "threw himself on the ground" and prayed earnestly that he might be spared the terrible ordeal about to unfold. "Yet, not what I want, but what you want," Jesus prayed. His desire to obey God and fulfill his own divine mandate was unwavering.

Mark also takes precious space in this shortest Gospel to tell about the sleepy disciples, Peter, James, and John. Jesus specifically told them that he was greatly distressed, distressed to the point of death, and he asked for their attentiveness and prayers. Not able to stay awake and support Jesus with their prayers, they fell asleep, oblivious to the growing anguish of Jesus. Three times, Jesus woke them up and repeated his request for their prayers. Three times, they fell asleep once again. It is a small story, seemingly unimportant in the tragedy that was soon to unfold. But it is a hint of the loneliness and isolation of Jesus' sufferings. Even his closest friends were not able to accompany him on his journey to the cross.

The trial of Jesus had at least two phases. First the religious authorities questioned him on charges of blasphemy. Witnesses were quickly assembled. Testimony was heard. When the testimonies did not agree with one another, a telltale sign that the proceedings were rigged, the high priest asked Jesus directly, "Are you the Messiah, the Son of the Blessed One?" Jesus responded, "I am" (Mark 14:61–62). Outraged at this proof of blasphemy, the chief priests pronounced him as deserving of death and allowed the soldiers to beat and torment Jesus.

It was in this surreal setting, a hastily convened, dead-of-night trial, that Peter betrayed Jesus. The same disciple who confidently stated earlier, "You are the Christ, the Son of the living God!" in the bright sunlight of Jesus' fame as a healer and teacher, now denied that he knew Jesus. When the rooster crowed the early morning to pale light, Peter suddenly remembered, to his shame and horror, Jesus' prediction of this very event. At that time, Peter thought the prediction was a sick joke. Now, when he realized his treachery, Peter broke down and wept. His heart would remain burdened with guilt and sorrow until after Jesus' resurrection, when Jesus would forgive Peter for his betrayal.

A sentence of capital punishment could only be handed down by the Roman governor of the province. Early in the morning, Jesus was transferred to Pilate, the governor of Judea. By this time, a crowd had formed, bent on Jesus' death. Knowing that a crowd mentality is dangerous and unpredictable, Pilate tried to dissuade the people from their murderous goal. The crowd refused to be appeased. Washing his hands of the whole situation, Pilate released Jesus to the crowd and ordered his execution. Once again, in the courtyard of the palace, Jesus was beaten and mocked.

Now, in the Gospel accounts, it seems that each hour is counted. The comments of people passing by are noted. The sign on Jesus' cross is identified, "This is Jesus, the King of the Jews." A brief exchange between Jesus and a thief crucified next to him is noted. Some of the people huddled at the scene of execution are identified, including Jesus' faithful women followers and the disciple John. Jesus' words from the cross are recorded. From noon until three in the afternoon, darkness falls over the land. Jesus cries out in a loud voice, "My God, my God, why have you forsaken me?" And then, suddenly, the end. Mark says, "Then Jesus gave a loud cry and breathed his last. And the curtain of the temple was torn in two, from top to bottom. Now when the centurion, who stood facing him, saw that in this way he breathed his last, he said, 'Truly this man was God's Son!'" (Mark 15:37–39).

Joseph of Arimathea, a high-level religious leader and a secret follower of Jesus, went to Pilate and asked for the body of Jesus, so that Jesus might receive a proper burial. When he was given permission, Joseph took the body of Jesus down from the cross, wrapped it in a linen burial cloth, and placed the body in his own family tomb, carved from solid rock. A large stone was rolled in front of the tomb and guards were stationed to prevent any further public disturbance. It seemed that the life and career of Jesus, prophet and teacher, had come to an end.

The Resurrection of Jesus

The early morning light had not yet broken over the horizon when the women hurried quietly to the place where Jesus was buried. Still dazed by the events of the days just passed, they were motivated only by a desire to do what simple good they could. Carrying spices for the slain body of Jesus, the women were determined to offer one final act of service and love to their Lord.

Their friend and teacher, Jesus of Nazareth, had been cruelly executed two days earlier. Accused of sedition and blasphemy, he had been condemned to die. They witnessed it all. They had heard the dull clunk of the stone as it rolled into place to close the entrance of the tomb where Jesus' body was laid. In the cool of the early morning, perhaps they still could not really believe it had all happened. But, remembering the horrors of the cross, it all came back again in grief still painfully sharp. Wondering aloud how the large stone might be rolled away from its place over the entrance, they approached the tomb.

The four Gospels differ in some of the details about what happened at the place of the tomb that early morning. Matthew reports that there was an earthquake, that an angel appeared like lightning, that the guards fainted with fear, and that the women heard from the angel the astonishing news that Jesus was raised from the dead. Hearing this, they ran with joy to tell the rest of the disciples. Mark's Gospel reports that the women were filled not with joy, but with fear and that they did not tell anyone the news. Luke says that the women found the tomb with the stone rolled away and went in to investigate. Suddenly, two angels appeared, dazzling them with their appearance. But when the women went to report this to the rest of the disciples, they were met with scoffing disbelief. According to John, Mary Magdalene alone went to the tomb while it was still dark, and saw an empty tomb with just the burial clothes lying there. She ran and got Peter and John, who came and looked. After they left, Jesus himself appeared to Mary, saw her grief, and spoke her name in comfort. Her joy, relief, and wonder knew no end.

Each Gospel account is slightly different in its details on the resurrection. But they all agree on the life-changing, heart-stopping importance of the resurrection of Jesus Christ. With the sun rising that morning, so rose the victory of God's love over sin and evil. The resurrection is the confirmation of Jesus Christ's life, ministry, and death. It is a sure sign that all creation will someday be restored to peace and harmony. It is the foundation of Christian faith everywhere. And it guarantees the resurrection of all believers to a life of eternal communion with God and with one another.

Looking back on the life and ministry of Jesus of Nazareth from the vantage point of the resurrection is a little bit like standing at the top of a mountain after a long and grueling hike. One instantly forgets the rigors of the climb because of the spectacular scenic vistas all around. Viewed from the resurrection, Jesus' identity as Lord and Savior seems obvious. But the disciples' experience was quite different. They knew Jesus as a beloved and respected teacher. Only gradually did they realize that this man was the Chosen One of God, the Messiah, their long-promised and long-awaited Lord. Even when faith dawned in the hearts of the disciples, it was a faith of stops and starts. In the light of the resurrection, the disciples and followers of Jesus finally understood what the angel had announced to Mary, many years earlier. This Jesus is the Christ, the Holy One, the Son of God.

Christian believers today have the benefit of looking at the cross of Jesus through their confidence in the resurrection. Although the cross looks like a terrible defeat, in the light of the resurrection it is really a convincing display of the love of God, willing to go even through death for the sake of the world. It is the end of the story that interprets everything that comes before. Like reading the last paragraph of a book before starting at the beginning, believers know that the resurrection of Jesus makes all the difference.

The Birth of the Church

Christian communities, from the first century to the twenty-first century, have always struggled to understand the death and resurrection of Jesus. Some of the earliest Christians, including the disciples and other faithful followers of Jesus, were actually present at the death of Jesus. They knew better than anyone the grim and grisly events of that day. That day certainly did not appear to be good news; it did not appear to be God's great saving act for all the world. The Gospel accounts, in fact, seem to show the disciples as terribly frightened, in hiding and defeated. In fact, the only people who showed some vague awareness that this particular death was much more than a political execution were the thief crucified next to Jesus and the centurion, one of his executioners. They both knew that Jesus was an innocent man, being put to death unjustly. "Jesus, remember me when you come into your kingdom," said the thief. "Surely this was a righteous man," said the centurion.

It was not until Easter morning, when the astonishing news of Jesus' resurrection came to the disciples from the women who had been at the tomb early in the morning, did the *saving* significance of Jesus' death begin to dawn on the disciples. The very first reflections on the meaning of Jesus' death and resurrection are recorded in Luke 24, when two followers of Jesus, perhaps a husband and wife, walked with the risen Jesus the seven miles from Jerusalem to the little town of Emmaus. They did not know it was Jesus at first. They shared with Jesus their dismay and grief over the events of the previous week. Jesus then explained the Hebrew Scriptures to them and demonstrated how it was necessary for the Messiah to suffer, die, and be raised to glory. It was not until they arrived home and invited Jesus to stay for supper that they suddenly recognized him. When he left later in the evening, they turned to each other and said, "Were not our hearts burning within us?" Perhaps this is the first word of Christian witness. The Emmaus couple had a powerful sense that this Jesus was the Lord, risen and revealed to them in the breaking of the bread at their humble dinner table. They hurried the seven long miles back to Jerusalem to announce to the gathered disciples their remarkable experience.

Jesus spent forty days with the disciples and other followers after his resurrection. He had long conversations with them, trying to explain to them the kingdom of God, a kingdom of peace and justice and reconciliation with God. Yet, amazingly, the disciples only understood these things dimly. The first chapter of the book of Acts reports that they were still expecting an earthly, political kingdom led by Jesus. They asked him, "Lord, is this the time when you will restore the kingdom to Israel?" (Acts 1:6). Even the resurrection did not correct their own set ideas of who Jesus was.

In response, Jesus simply told them this was none of their business: "It is not for you to know the times or periods that the Father has set by his own authority" (Acts 1:7). And then he made a promise that was to change everything. "But you will receive power when the Holy Spirit has come upon you; and you will be my witnesses in Jerusalem, in all Judea and Samaria, and to the ends of the earth" (Acts 1:8). Jesus promised to send the Holy Spirit to give them the wisdom, the courage, and the power required to proclaim the good news of Jesus all over the world.

After this, Jesus was taken up into heaven, leaving the disciples behind in wide-eyed and open-mouthed amazement. In the story of Jesus' ascending into heaven in Acts 1, two angels appear and ask the disciples, "Why are you standing there looking up toward heaven?" The angels seem to imply that staring at the sky was not the disciples' first order of business. Now, they were to wait for the coming of the Spirit.

The day of Pentecost, the day when the promised Holy Spirit was poured out on the gathered disciples, is the birthday of the Christian church. The Holy Spirit's dramatic arrival finally gave the disciples the eyes of faith to see. No more did they question the identity of Jesus. No more did they agitate for a political uprising. No more did they demand proofs and signs. The Holy Spirit filled them with the joy and confidence of the gospel.

Pentecost morning, when the Holy Spirit was poured out on the church, was a noisy and chaotic event. Luke tells us in Acts 2 that all the disciples "were filled with the Holy Spirit and began to speak in other languages, as the Spirit gave them ability." Pentecost was an event so startling, so strange, that bystanders that morning assumed the disciples were all drunk. Far from disturbing the peace, however, they began proclaiming the peace, the peace of Christ. Peter's sermon on Pentecost day proclaimed with confidence that Jesus is both Lord and Christ. When the people responded with fear, Peter instructed them, "Repent, and be baptized every one of you in the name of Jesus Christ so that your sins may be forgiven; and you will receive the gift of the Holy Spirit" (Acts 2:38).

Some days later, Peter declared to the respected elders and teachers of the law, "There is salvation in no one else, for there is no other name under heaven given among mortals by which we must be saved" (Acts 4:12). The stories of the growth of the early church in Acts give us a clear impression that within days after the Holy Spirit was poured out on the disciples, the message was being proclaimed to anyone who would listen—Jesus Christ is Lord and Savior.

2

A Gallery of Portraits: What Can
We Know about Jesus?

Most Christians, if asked whether the Bible gives them any information about Jesus, would respond, "Of course. The Bible is full of stories about Jesus." So recent controversy over what the Bible actually does tell us about Jesus strikes some people as strange. The stories are all there, plain to see. Other people are fascinated by the flurry of recent biblical scholarship on the Gospel accounts of Jesus that calls into question the reliability of the Gospel records of Jesus' life. They are curious about the current discussion among biblical scholars about the four Gospels, and want to know what other ancient documents reveal about Jesus, such as the documents that archaeologists have only recently discovered in the Middle East.

Although some biblical scholars have caught the spotlight of media attention quite recently, vigorous discussion on what the Bible reliably tells us about Jesus has been going on for about two hundred years. In the past fifteen years, this discussion has intensified, attracting the attention of large numbers of interested laypeople and nonspecialists. They wonder about what kind of person Jesus, son of Mary and Joseph, first-century itinerant teacher and healer, was. Did he *really* perform miracles? Did he *really* rise from the dead? Did he *really* ascend into heaven? All these questions cluster around the big question of "the historical Jesus."

New Testament scholars have long known that the four Gospels are not biographical documents in the usual sense.

The Gospels do not attempt to record the "life and times" of Jesus Christ. They do not pretend to be a complete archive of the mighty deeds of Jesus. The Gospels do not even say much about the personality of Jesus. Unlike modern biographies, which concentrate on character and setting and chronology and context, the Gospels show little interest in such matters. Nothing is mentioned about Jesus' physical appearance, and, with the exception of just a few comments about his compassion, anger, or exhaustion, the Gospels do not much concern themselves with Jesus' emotions. Very little is included about Jesus' childhood. Almost nothing exists about his family. Besides his disciples, only a few friends are mentioned, and these friends are mostly women, Mary and Martha of Bethany, Mary Magdalene, and other women followers.

Countless readers of the Bible have noticed that each of the four Gospels tells the story of Jesus in quite a distinctive way. Mark's depiction of Jesus is noticeably unlike John's depiction, for example. Mark's Jesus is earthy and feisty. He gets angry, tired, and hungry. John's Jesus is ethereal and mystical. Matthew's Jesus is a Jewish Jesus, tracing his ancestry back to father Abraham and constantly correcting the Jewish leaders and his own disciples on the deeper meaning of the traditional Jewish law. Luke's Jesus is a healer and social critic. The variety and difference of perspective in the four Gospels is not unlike the common experience we have in listening to the story of a car accident or a quarrel between children. The same event can sound quite different, depending on the perspective of the reporter.

An additional complication of the four Gospels is that some specific stories are told not only with a unique perspective, but varying in particular details. In John's Gospel, Mary Magdalene was the first person to come to the tomb. She then ran and summoned Peter and "the other disciple," often assumed to be John himself. In Mark and Luke, a group of women are named as the first witnesses to the resurrection. In Matthew, two women, Mary Magdalene and "the other Mary" are identified.

The Sermon on the Mount in the Gospel of Matthew is different from that in the Gospel of Luke. In Matthew, Jesus "went up the mountain, and . . . began to speak," giving the first beatitude,

"Blessed are the poor in spirit, for theirs is the kingdom of heaven" (Matt. 5:3). In Luke Jesus "came down" from the mountain and "stood on a level place," saying, "Blessed are you who are poor, for yours is the kingdom of God" (Luke 6:17, 20). Luke portrays Jesus here as referring specifically to poor people, while Matthew seems to portray Jesus as advocating a certain attitude of humility or meekness for all.

Whether a preacher chooses to preach the Luke account of the Sermon on the Mount or the Matthew account can say a lot. Perhaps well-heeled, socially and economically secure congregations don't much want to hear about the poor inheriting the kingdom of God. They might prefer a nice reminder about humility. Oppressed peoples, however, hear Jesus' words in Luke as a vigorous affirmation of God's "preferential option for the poor." This famous phrase was coined in Medellín, Colombia, in 1968, at a conference of liberation theologians. It quickly became a short summary statement of liberation theology in the last third of the twentieth century. Luke's version of the Sermon on the Mount is understood by liberation theologians as a vigorous prophetic command to uphold the cause of the poor. Clearly, the differences between the two Gospel accounts is no small matter.

Differences between the Gospel accounts of Jesus' life, teaching, death, and resurrection have caused anxiety among some people, and curious questions among others. Given the unique nature of each Gospel record of Jesus, can we learn anything reliable about Jesus from the Gospels?

As might be expected, there is a wide variety of answers to this question. Some biblical scholars have labored in an attempt to uncover the definitive "life of Jesus" based on the Gospel sources. They try to determine which sayings of Jesus are authentic, for instance, and which are not. They try to find the "true core" of the Gospels. Other scholars are not so interested in what is actual fact in the Gospels. They believe the Gospels are not a record of facts at all, but the personal response of the Gospel writers to the person and message of Jesus. The past two hundred years can be divided into three somewhat distinct "quests for the historical Jesus," each with its own unique characteristics and concerns. In each case, the fuss and furor over these "quests for the historical Jesus" was considerable.

The First Quest

The first quest for the historical Jesus took place about two hundred years ago and centered in Europe, especially Germany. New Testament scholar N. T. Wright, in his book *Who Was Jesus?* asks us to imagine these early "questers" as artists, each painting a portrait of Jesus and hanging the portrait in a large art gallery. One portrait is of a disappointed, failed Jesus—a prophet whose vision was cruelly ended on the cross. Another portrait is of a revolutionary Jesus—a wild prophet who had grand political ambitions. Yet another portrait shows a misty, romantic Jesus—a Jesus meek and mild, whose message of love drew large, hopeful crowds. Still another portrait depicts a philosopher Jesus—a wise sage who preached justice, peace, and the Golden Rule.

Many portraits of Jesus had been added to this imaginary gallery, most claiming to represent the "real" Jesus. Some of the portraits are covered with dust, cobwebs clouding their images. Some look quaint and old-fashioned. N. T. Wright then invites us to picture what happens: "Now imagine a man, with wild hair and flashing eyes, bursting into the room. He rushes round, tearing the portraits from the walls as though in a frenzy. He smashes the glass in the frames and tramples on the paintings with his dirty boots."[1] In one swift move, this intruder tore all the old portraits of Jesus off the gallery walls and replaced them with his own dramatic sketch, a rough charcoal drawing of a fiery-eyed prophet tacked onto the wall where the elegant paintings had been. This wild man in N.T. Wright's fantasy scene was Albert Schweitzer, a brilliant scholar, musician, and, eventually, missionary doctor to Africa.

Schweitzer was in no way a wild person himself; he was a man of great dignity and seriousness. But the impact of his 1906 book, *The Quest of the Historical Jesus,* was stunning. He brilliantly showed that all the nineteenth-century portraits of Jesus ignored

[1] Luke Timothy Johnson, *The Real Jesus* (San Francisco: HarperSanFrancisco, 1996), 1.

the Jewish context of Jesus and made him look a lot like a nineteenth-century European intellectual. In fact, he said, the whole nineteenth-century effort to discover the historical Jesus was a prolonged scene of "boundless confusion."[2] A later twentieth-century biblical scholar, Rudolf Schnackenburg, agreed with Schweitzer when he said that all the strenuous research was "bound to fail, because the Gospels are simply not historical writings, strictly speaking. Rather, they are documents that immediately draw history into the faith-picture of Jesus Christ."[3]

In other words, the first quest, very roughly dated from 1800 to 1900, simply asked the wrong questions. It asked, "What happened exactly, and how can we be sure?" A better question asked of the Gospel accounts of Jesus would be, "Who is this Jesus, and who is he calling us to be?" The Gospels do not answer the sorts of historically precise questions the nineteenth-century questers were pursuing.

The enormous controversy stirred up by the nineteenth-century quest was not confined to academic seminar rooms and lecture halls. These matters stirred the passions of preachers and laypeople, ordinary Christians who felt their Bible was being taken away from them. Devout and sincere Christians felt threatened when scholarly books questioned the biblical accounts of the miracles of Jesus and his bodily resurrection. One minister wrote an anguished letter to a professor about one of these books, confessing that it had robbed him of his peace of mind. The professor wrote back, reassured him, and then said, "I hope that after the experience which you have had you will for the future refrain from reading books of this kind, which are not written for you, and of which there is no necessity for you to take any notice."[4] The anguished believer probably received little comfort from this advice.

Not only did faithful Christian believers feel at risk in the flurry of books that appeared in the nineteenth century. The conse-

---

[2] Albert Schweitzer, *The Quest of the Historical Jesus,* trans. W. Montgomery from the first German edition, *Von Reimarus zu Wrede* (New York: Macmillan Co., 1968), 9.

[3] Rudolf Schnackenburg, *Jesus in the Gospels: A Biblical Christology,* trans. O. C. Dean (Louisville, Ky.: Westminster John Knox Press, 1995), 5.

[4] This anonymous exchange of letters is reported by Schweitzer, 100.

quences could be devastating to the questers themselves. One of the most controversial writers was a young German scholar named David Strauss. When he was just twenty-seven years old, he published his famous, or infamous, *The Life of Jesus*. In this 1835 book, Strauss denied the supernatural elements of the Gospels, claiming that the Gospel accounts of Jesus' miracles were legends or stories that developed among early Christians. The reaction of the public and the academy was swift. He was fired from his teaching position at Tübingen University. His scholarly reputation never recovered. His friends abandoned him. Toward the end of his life, he remarked, "I might well bear a grudge against my book, for it has done me much evil."[5]

In the place of what he considered inadequate portraits of Jesus, Strauss's included, Schweitzer proposed a radical Jesus. Here was a Jesus who believed the world was shortly going to come to an end. Jesus' preaching, according to Schweitzer, was filled with dire warnings and stern calls to repentance. There was fire in the eyes of Schweitzer's Jesus. What made Schweitzer's portrait of Jesus so stunning is that, for him, Jesus was a failure. Jesus' fervent message of apocalyptic gloom and doom did not happen. Jesus is, as Albert Schweitzer concluded in his book, "a stranger and an enigma."[6]

In fact, Schweitzer is convinced that believers should abandon any hopes of finding a secure historical foundation for the faith. He states that Jesus as a concrete, historical person is not only unknowable, but irrelevant to Christian faith. The only thing that really matters is the "spirit which goes forth" from Jesus. It is that "spirit" which gives us the vision to work for a better world. Schweitzer's lack of interest in the historical facts of Jesus' life is puzzling to some readers. They determine that *The Quest for the Historical Jesus* offers little by way of support and affirmation of Christian belief.

It is true that Schweitzer would insist that it is a waste a time to fuss about the facts of Jesus' life, the words he did or did not actually utter, the precise scientific explanations of his resurrection or birth.

---

[5] Schweitzer, *The Quest*, 5.
[6] Schweitzer, *The Quest*, 399.

The importance of Schweitzer's book is its vigorous emphasis that what is crucially important is how the spirit of Jesus changes people's lives and calls them to live in truth, integrity, honesty, and service. A Christian faith that does not make an impact in the world is a poor gospel indeed.

The Quest of the Historical Jesus summarized over one hundred years of searching for the historical evidence for Jesus, his miracles, the resurrection, and other events portrayed in the Gospels. This century of scholarly questing produced a whole spectrum of very different pictures, including Schweitzer's own "charcoal sketch" that portrayed Jesus as a wild-eyed, delusional prophet. Schweitzer's book marked the end of the "first quest." No longer was it possible to read the Gospels as "newspaper" accounts of what Jesus said and what he did. Instead, deep questions arose about what sort of books the Gospels are. Do they give us reliable information about Jesus? Can we really understand who Jesus was as a first-century Jewish teacher? Put bluntly, are the Gospels fact or fiction?

The Second Quest

In the 1950s, new effort was made to come to grips with these questions. German New Testament scholar Rudolf Bultmann (1884–1976) was a major influence in the second quest. He was convinced that the interest in questions about the historical Jesus was a blind alley. Those issues just aren't important, said Bultmann. What is important is the continuing significance of Jesus for Christian belief today. "Never mind about what Jesus did and what he said! We can't know that anyway! Just believe and be transformed by the faith that has risen up within you," Bultmann might say.

In effect, Bultmann moved away from the historical events of Jesus' life altogether, taking interest instead in the proclamation of the gospel and what difference that made in the lives of early Christians. He said that the Bible clearly assumes an obsolete three-story universe, with heaven, earth, and hell. Those mythological assumptions must be discarded and the "real" meaning of the gospel recovered. In reaction to this radical move away from history by Bultmann and his followers, the "second quest" for the historical Jesus began.

In the early 1950s, Ernst Käsemann, a German scholar, focused his attention not on the historical reliability of Gospel events, but on the words of Jesus. Notice that this "new quest" concentrated on the sayings of Jesus rather than on what sort of person Jesus was or what he did. No new portraits were hung in the old dusty gallery of Jesus portraits. Instead, the focus was on the words of Jesus. A set of criteria was suggested for how to make a respectable conclusion about the words of Jesus. One of these criteria was the "dissimilarity criterion." A saying of Jesus was considered authentic if it did *not* fit into the context of first-century Judaism. It was suggested that the Gospel accounts were probably revised by a succession of editors, tidying up the narrative and making Jesus' words sound more like his Jewish context. So, it was thought, if a saying of Jesus did not quite "fit," that was probably a saying that survived the editor's pen and was more likely to be authentic.

Another issue of interest to these scholars in the middle of the twentieth century was the self-understanding of Jesus. Did Jesus know that he was the Son of God? the Messiah? the Savior of the world? There was a great deal of diversity in this very loosely grouped "second quest" around these questions of Jesus' self-understanding and the authenticity of the words of Jesus. Some scholars concluded that Jesus became more and more aware of his messianic identity, that he knew he had a unique relationship with God, that he knew he would have to suffer and die but would return in glory to his Father in heaven.[7] Other scholars were doubtful about these conclusions and continued to approach the Gospels from a more skeptical approach, following Bultmann.

The Third Quest

Of course, one major problem with the project of the second questers—to scrutinize the words of Jesus according to a list of

---

[7] These include Martin Hengel, James Dunn, I. H. Marshall, and D. F. C. Moule.

criteria—is that the words of Jesus are viewed from the outset with suspicion and doubt. The official list of authentic words of Jesus is continually shrinking under this predominantly negative bias.

Since the late 1970s, a noticeable stream of scholars is clearing a new path for biblical scholarship. Some of these scholars, such as E. P. Sanders and Geza Vermes, are leaving behind an exclusive interest in the words of Jesus and are refocusing interest in the Jewishness of Jesus. The context of Jesus in a first-century Jewish Palestine is studied; the sorts of cultural influences at work in that place at that time are studied. This interest in *context* is what gives much of recent biblical scholarship its unique character. Some see this as a third quest.

A lively and controversial group of recent scholars has generated a great deal of publicity in the late 1980s and 1990s. Known as the Jesus Seminar, the members are notorious, in part, for the way they come to their conclusions, voting on the most authentic and least authentic words of Jesus. The Jesus Seminar is an interesting blend of the characteristics of the second quest and the third quest. Their strong interest in the authentic words of Jesus continues the second quest. Their equally vital interest in the Jewish context, as well as the Greek and Roman background of Jesus' life, gives their work the flavor of the third quest. The Jesus Seminar is a good reminder that intellectual movements cannot be neatly boxed and labeled.

In spite of the wide publicity that has greeted the Jesus Seminar, their work does not represent the mainstream of biblical scholarship. The members of the group have demonstrated their ability to sell books and attract sound-bite media coverage, but they do not represent the long tradition of Christian reflection. They do not speak for vast numbers of ordinary Christian believers. They are, in fact, a distinct, idiosyncratic minority voice. Even so, because they attract such interest, because they have published so many books, because several of them lecture widely, because they do challenge the assumptions of many people on who Jesus is, some further consideration is necessary.

The members of the Jesus Seminar who have gained the most public recognition are John Dominic Crossan, Marcus Borg, and

Robert Funk. These are the names frequently seen on posters in church basements advertising a public lecture. The lectures bear titles like "Can We Really Know Anything about Jesus?" These are the people television networks or magazine editors often contact for a quick quote that can be used in a special report.

One of the goals of the Jesus Seminar was to give a verdict on the probability of each reported saying of Jesus in the Gospel accounts. What excited the imaginations of the media was the method of the group's decision. The members cast their votes using colored beads. A red bead meant a definitive authentic saying of Jesus. A pink bead indicated a saying that sounds like something Jesus would say. A gray bead indicates real doubt—probably Jesus did not speak those words. A black bead was a thumbs down—Jesus could not possibly have said it.

Academic professionals who are accustomed to being completely ignored by the secular media must admit a sort of admiration for scholars who manage to garner wide media coverage. But important questions remain: What are the results of the Jesus Seminar? Are these results valid? Are they in continuity with the long Christian tradition? Are they respectful of deep Christian instincts about Jesus?

The results of the Jesus Seminar were presented to the public in 1993 with the publication of *The Five Gospels*.[8] This book was a retranslation of the four Gospels in the New Testament plus the Gospel of Thomas, an ancient document discovered in 1947 with some similarities to the four Gospels, but one that did not become recognized early in the church's history as belonging in the New Testament. The retranslation of the four biblical Gospels is often startling. Jesus says in the Beatitudes, "Congratulations, you poor!" instead of "Blessed are the poor." In addition, *The Five Gospels* reported the results of the colored-bead voting. Not much of the words of Jesus remained after this process. Only a dozen or so sayings of Jesus were considered authentic by the Jesus Seminar.

---

[8] Robert W. Funk, Roy W. Hoover, and the Jesus Seminar, *The Five Gospels: The Search for the Authentic Words of Jesus: New Translation and Commentary* (New York: Macmillan Publishing Co., 1993).

Reaction to the Jesus Seminar has been very mixed in congregations. Some churches hold well-attended weekend seminars on *The Five Gospels*. Other churches do not want anything to do with this fad. In general, reaction in academic circles to the Jesus Seminar has been negative. The scholarship does not meet the standards of discipline and clarity prized by biblical scholars.

Some scholars, however, note with appreciation at least one effect of the Jesus Seminar: laypeople have become fascinated with important questions about the historical Jesus, about the Gospel accounts of Jesus, about who the "real Jesus" is. Some laypeople have been so intrigued with the Jesus Seminar that they are reflecting once again on the classic Christian claims about Jesus. They have discovered that their own understandings of Jesus are too much influenced by their own cultural setting. They are grateful to learn about the Jewish context of Jesus.

This is a good thing. But the negative bias of the Jesus Seminar toward classical understandings of the faith are too obvious to ignore. All classic and traditional understandings of Jesus are simply assumed by these writers to be quaint, foolishly naive, even oppressive. The Nicene Creed, for example, a fourth-century statement of Christian belief, is dismissed as tyrannical and authoritarian.[9]

This attitude reveals a deeply entrenched presupposition of the Jesus Seminar, that the "real Jesus" is not the same as the Jesus worshiped by Christian believers for many centuries. Robert Funk and the other members seem to approach their task of evaluating the words of Jesus assuming that the "real Jesus" is someone quite different. The Seminar is clearly negative toward many forms of traditional piety and belief. Christians who are confident in the truth and meaning of traditional Christian belief wish that a disclaimer could be printed on the cover of the Jesus Seminar books: "The views contained in this book are not necessarily those of countless millions of Christian believers today and throughout the ages." One sharp critic of the Jesus Seminar proceedings registers his own discomfort on the slapdash style that sometimes has characterized the group: "The most irritating feature of the Seminar

---

[9] Funk, et al., *The Five Gospels,* 7–8.

may have been its indulgence in cute and casual discourse concerning matters of considerable historical moment and genuine religious concern."[10]

The effects of popularizing this kind of slapdash scholarship are sometimes very serious. Far more than a tempest in an academic teapot, the Jesus Seminar's easy dismissals have influenced some people to conclude that the Christian faith is a sham, a sheer invention. For these people, the "expertise" of these professors is trusted. The very possibility of Christian identity and belief is called into question. For others, a massive reduction of the big claims of the Christian faith occurs. They begin to think that Jesus is not the Word of God made flesh for us and our salvation. Instead, Jesus was just another itinerant sage. If this is the effect of the Jesus Seminar, clearly, other voices are badly needed in the discussion. The voices of confidence and trust in the Scripture, in Jesus Christ whom the Scripture reveals, and in the accumulated wisdom of the Christian tradition need to challenge and correct the current fascination with the Jesus Seminar.

The Gospel in Four Forms

After two hundred years of intensive questing for the historical Jesus, what conclusions can thoughtful Christians draw? What *does* the Bible tells us about Jesus? Some Christians have followed current scholarship, such as the Jesus Seminar, and concluded that the Bible tells us almost nothing. After all, noted scholars have told us that the text of the Bible is nothing but a complex jumble of editings, compilations, deletions, and insertions. We can gather no solid data about Jesus there at all. Other Christians have rejected both the methods and the results of all modern biblical scholarship. They firmly clutch their red-letter Bibles and insist that Jesus said every word indicated in red ink. They do not want any scholar or preacher taking away *their* Bible. The Bible says it, and that is good enough for them.

These two extreme reactions, fortunately, are not the only choices

---

[10] Johnson, *The Real Jesus,* 15.

open to thoughtful Christians. It is quite possible, for example, to recognize the fascinating insights of the best biblical scholarship about the unique context and historical setting of the Gospels and yet trust the Gospels as reliable sources for learning about Jesus. It is quite possible to read contemporary biblical scholarship with interest and openness, but also with judiciousness and care.

Not everything that has been published in recent years is worthy of serious consideration. Sensational accounts of the life of Jesus sometimes grab headlines but should not shake the confidence of Christians in the basic trustworthiness of Scripture. The Gospels, it is true, do not begin to match standards of verifiable biography. But the purpose of the Gospels' accounts of Jesus is not merely to narrate events. Their purpose is to tell the story that has changed the whole world, to convince the reader that Jesus is the Christ, the Son of the living God, to motivate the reader to faith and service, to comfort the reader in times of grief.

In the face of controversy in the scholarly community concerning the authenticity of the sayings of Jesus and the reliability of the Gospel record of Jesus, some perspective is needed. One biblical scholar helps set this perspective in saying, "We have to be thankful that we have the four Gospels, each of which from its own viewpoint brings us close to the person of Jesus."[11] The four accounts of the resurrection, the two accounts of the Sermon on the Mount (or Sermon on the Plain), the numerous small discrepancies between miracle stories—these are not threats to the faith of Christians. Rather, they all portray Jesus from the unique viewpoint of the particular Gospel.

Even early Christians noticed and appreciated this fact. Irenaeus of Lyon (d. ca. 202 C.E.) once said the four Gospels are "the gospel in four forms."[12] There is *one* gospel concerning Jesus Christ. This gospel is proclaimed by the four Gospel traditions in ways that are unique and particular. To the question, "Well, what is the *truth*? Did Jesus' sermon take place on the mountain or on the plain?" we might say, "We don't know." We might then add, "But nothing cru-

---

[11] Rudolf Schnackenburg, *Jesus in the Gospels,* 323.
[12] *Adv. Haereses 3.11.8.*

cial rests on us knowing this. And our uncertainty on this point does not compromise in the least our trust in the love of God through Jesus Christ our Lord."

Christians can rightly be confident in the Scriptures because God has chosen, through the power of the Holy Spirit, to use this book to reveal Jesus to us and to form and shape us into the community that is the body of Christ. There is nothing about the Bible, on its own, that elevates it to the status of the Word of God for the church. Its poetry is not so lovely, its stories not so dramatic, its sayings not so wise that, by these things alone, it deserves to be called God's Word. Rather, the Bible is the Word of God because, by the Spirit, we meet Jesus in the Bible. The Spirit illuminates our minds, enlivens our hearts, and moves us out into the world. It is the Holy Spirit, ultimately, that guarantees the Scriptures for the faith of the church.

3

Treasure in Clay Pots: What Does the Church Say about Jesus?

A sign on a church lawn proclaims, "No Creed but Christ." A believer remarks to a friend, "Believing in Jesus is enough for me. I don't need any *doctrine*." Traditional creeds and confessions are often rejected as musty archives or quaint antiques—orthodoxy is oppressive. Clearly, the reputation of doctrine is badly tarnished for many contemporary people.

This is partially due to the way doctrine has been used in the church. In the early centuries of the church, priests and bishops were sometimes banished if their theological views did not meet a standard of acceptable belief. That standard of acceptable belief at times reversed itself, depending on who happened to have political or ecclesiastical power, making the banished bishop once again welcome in town. Throughout the history of the church, disagreements over doctrine have led to schism and religious wars. After the particularly vicious Thirty Years War in Germany in the seventeenth century, some early Enlightenment writers denounced religion altogether. Outraged at the social chaos that followed religious conflict, they concluded that religion was barbaric.

There is no doubt that sometimes doctrine has been used as a weapon of exclusion. Disagreements over doctrine have led to persecution, execution, war, banishment, torture, and excommunication. The church has been remarkably slow to learn the lessons of unity, conversation, and hospitality. This fact alone steers some people straight away from the door of the church.

At other times, doctrine has been excessively tidy and exact. There are textbooks of theology that list the nine reasons why God created the world, the twelve attributes or characteristics of God, the exact number of people who will live to all eternity in heaven. The excessive fussiness of some doctrine gives the impression that this is all sheer invention—all style, no substance.

Sometimes, doctrine has ironed out the mystery of God and reduced magnificence to minutiae. In the Old Testament book of Job, there is a dramatic scene when God speaks to Job out of the whirlwind. "Were you there, Job," God says, "when I created the heavens, the great beasts of the sea, the soaring birds of the air? Were you there when I set the boundaries of the seas and the foundations of the earth? Were you?" (Job 38–41). Job, overwhelmed by the majesty and greatness of God, answered in awe, "I have uttered what I did not understand, things too wonderful for me, which I did not know" (Job 42:3). Doctrine sometimes forgets its proper humility. Sometimes it speaks of what it does not know. God is greater than all human speech. God cannot be captured and controlled by any human speech. Words about God must never pretend to replace the living God.

But doctrine has also fed the life of Christians and formed them in their knowledge of God. Uncounted millions of words throughout the two thousand years of Christian faith have spilled onto paper in an attempt to state the truth of God's self-revelation in the Bible and in Jesus Christ. Some of these words are called *creeds*. Creeds are statements that express the faith. The most famous creed is the Apostles' Creed, recited by Christians all over the world, in hundreds of languages. Whenever we stand and recite the Apostles' Creed, we join in a great chorus of faith that includes believers from Chicago, Santiago, Seoul, Cape Town, Amsterdam, Beijing, and scores of communities whose names we have never heard. The people who stand and recite the Apostles' Creed in their own language are our brothers and sisters in the faith, united with us by the Holy Spirit and heirs with us to all the promises of God.

Another way to express the Christian faith in words is through a *confession*. Similar to creeds, but usually longer, they too attempt to express the truth of the faith at a particular time and particular place. The sixteenth-century Reformation was a time when several important confessions were written by Protestant Reformers. Some of these include the Lutheran Augsburg Confession, written by Philipp Melanchthon, and the French Confession of 1559, written by John Calvin and the French Protestant Church. Another confession well known to many Presbyterians is the seventeenth-century Westminster Confession, a document that was forged in the heat of an impending civil war in England in the mid-1600s.

At their best, creeds and confessions encourage believers in times of persecution. At their best, they put into words, however faulty and limited, the truth of the gospel. The good news of the gospel—that in Jesus Christ, God is reconciled to the world and will accomplish a full restoration of shalom, of peace, in God's future—this good news must be spoken, explained, and taught. It is not, after all, written in some universally recognizable language in the stars. The treasure of the gospel must be spoken in the clay pots of human words, in language. This is what doctrine is—it is the truth of the gospel expressed in words in the teaching of the church.

What doctrine is *like* has intrigued many people. Is doctrine like a package dropped down to believers from heaven? Is it like an elaborate Lego structure, put together carefully from smaller pieces so that it all fits together? Is it like a plant, which grows from a seed, buds, and then bursts into full flower? Is it like the operating system of a computer, required for the faith to boot up? Is it like a yardstick, which measures all statements about God?

These sorts of questions perhaps interest only theologians and exceptionally curious people. But the question of what doctrine is and what good it does is important to the story of the church. Soon after Jesus Christ ascended into heaven and the Holy Spirit was poured out, Christians faced some basic dilemmas. The fact was that Jews and Gentiles in large numbers were coming to believe in Jesus. Jewish Christians, however, found it hard to accept the fact that God included Gentiles as well the covenant people of Israel in divine, gracious love. Gentile Christians, for their part, had little interest in following the ancient traditions of the Jews. The fundamental issue of what it meant to be a follower of Jesus became a pressing concern.

The story of Peter in Acts 10 is an example of this first crisis in the infant church. One day Peter was praying on the roof of a house where he was staying in Joppa, on the Mediterranean Sea. In his prayers, he experienced a dramatic vision. He saw the heavens open and an enormous sheet, held by four corners, was lowered to the ground. In the sheet was a small zoo—all kinds of animals, reptiles, and birds. Peter was born and raised in accordance with Jewish restrictions against the eating of certain animals. These were precisely the animals contained in this huge sheet. The text says, "Then he heard a voice saying, 'Get up, Peter; kill and eat.' But Peter said, 'By no means, Lord; for I have never eaten anything that is profane or unclean.' The voice said to him again, a second time, 'What God has made clean, you must not call profane'" (Acts 10:13–15).

Peter woke from his trance, puzzling over this strange vision. Just then, messengers sent by Cornelius, the Roman centurion from Caesarea, knocked on Peter's door. They informed Peter that Cornelius wished to see Peter. It was a two-day walk to Caesarea, but Peter knew he must go. When he met the Roman commander, Peter learned that Cornelius, too, had experienced a strange vision. In this dream, an angel appeared to Cornelius, instructing him to send for Peter. Now, finally, Peter and Cornelius, face to face, would learn the full reach and scope of the gospel. Peter realized that God's grace and forgiveness was intended not only for the Jews, the chosen people, but reached out to include all people. God's love was intended even for Cornelius, a Roman soldier, a member of the resented occupying army in Israel. This was unheard of, absolutely unthinkable.

But the truth of God's expansive love was unmistakable. Peter saw the long reach of God's love standing right before him in the person of Cornelius. After Cornelius explained the visit of the angel, Peter responded. What he said was, in one respect, a doctrine. Peter stated, in words, what the truth of the gospel means. He said, "I truly understand that God shows no partiality, but in every nation anyone who fears him and does what is right is acceptable to him" (Acts 10:34–35). The early Christians had to think through the implications of their belief in Jesus Christ as the Messiah, the Promised One. They had to learn that believing in Jesus meant that God does not play favorites.

When Peter said, "I truly understand that God shows no partiality," he was engaged in thinking through his belief in Jesus and putting it into words. Peter's statement is a small creed, a brief doctrinal statement. It illustrates that doctrine can do better than divide, reject, and oppress. At its best, it can clarify, empower, and liberate.

Doctrine about Jesus became a pressing concern for the church in the first few centuries. The young church experienced resistance from the Jews and from the wider culture. Jews accused Christians of believing in more than one God. When Jews noticed Christians worshiping Jesus, they concluded that Christians were polytheists, people who worship multiple gods. The political authorities criticized, and sometimes persecuted, Christians as well. They feared the growing numbers and potential political power of this religious movement. Other people accused Christians of being lax and immoral. After all, Christians proclaimed the free grace of God, a divine love that does not demand strict adherence to a list of requirements. Yet others accused the early church of teaching strange and outrageous myths—about a cross and an empty tomb. Some even accused them of cannibalism: it was well known that Christians spoke frankly about eating and drinking the body and blood of Christ in the Lord's Supper. Failing completely to understand the sacramental and symbolic nature of the Lord's Supper, the critics drew bizarre conclusions.

So doctrine became necessary for the early church as a way of explaining what it believed about Jesus. It was required as a way of refuting inaccurate understandings of the faith. It was a way of marking off Christian belief from alternative religious systems of the day. Doctrine was faith seeking understanding, belief finding voice.

Telling the complete story of the growth of doctrine in the church over two thousand years through a wide array of languages, cultures, personalities, influences, and crises is a task well beyond this book. But a couple of key turning points in the church's thinking about Jesus Christ are important.

The Stunning Claim That Jesus Is Divine

Christians in the first few centuries of the church gathered together around the reading of the Scriptures, both the Old Testament and the New Testament, which was then very new indeed. The four Gospels, assorted letters of Paul and Peter, and several other documents gradually became gathered together and recognized as the very word of God to the church. Communities of Christians also celebrated the Lord's Supper together, baptized new converts, and encouraged and supported one another in times of persecution and oppression. Most importantly, these Christians worshiped God. Their prayers of praise and intercession, however, were addressed not only to God, the one God, maker of heaven and earth. They were also addressed to Jesus Christ. Christians worshiped Jesus. The earliest, and shortest, creed in the New Testament proclaimed, "Jesus Christ is Lord" (Phil. 2:11).

The question of whether Christians worshiped one God or two gods or three gods had become a pressing issue already in the first few centuries of the church. Christian thinkers denied that they were polytheists. But it was not until the fourth and fifth centuries that a full doctrine was formulated in order to express as precisely as possible what worshiping Jesus implied. Ultimately, the Christian doctrine of the Trinity emerged, the doctrine that states that Jesus Christ is fully God, along with God the Father and God the Holy Spirit.

The doctrine of the Trinity answered the critics of the Christian faith. Contrary to their accusations, Christians are not polytheists. The Father, the Son, and the Holy Spirit are not three gods, but one God in three persons. The doctrine of the Trinity expresses the conviction that Jesus is God. Not just a really good person. Not a junior god. But true God become human.[1]

The doctrine of the Trinity was sparked by controversy. Around 320 C.E., an experienced clergyman by the name of Arius, almost near the end of a long and distinguished career, was serving a church in Alexandria, Egypt. Arius began to promote teachings

[1] See Philip Butin's book, *The Trinity* (Louisville, Ky.: Geneva Press, 2001), another in this Foundations of Christian Faith series.

about Jesus that created uneasiness in some of his colleagues. Although he was almost seventy years old, Arius was persistent in his views, ignored the concerns of his friends, and began to gather supporters to his cause.

Arius was convinced that Jesus was not God. Jesus was godlike, but not God. His reasoning was quite simple. Only God is absolutely transcendent and unique. There is no one like God. Only God is uncreated. Everything else has been created. From these few basic principles, Arius concluded that Jesus was created by God. This meant that, as Arius explained to a friend in a letter, "Before he was begotten or created or ordained or founded, he was not." This cluster of views became known as Arianism.

It was those three words, "he was not" that most alarmed Arius's opponents. They quickly saw that, according to Arius, at some point in time Jesus, the Son of God, did not exist. At some fixed point in time, the Son or Word of God was created. If the Word of God, become human in Jesus of Nazareth, is a creature, created in time by God, then it makes no sense to worship Jesus. Only God deserves to be worshiped and praised. Arius's views on Jesus made nonsense out of Christian worship.

In the same letter, Arius expressed his indignation that he was being hounded by his opponents. He was mystified by the traditional insistence that the Son of God has eternally existed with God. Arius thought that it was quite good enough to say that Jesus is "*like* God," not that Jesus *is* God. So he judged his opponents as the real heretics, commenting that "we cannot bear even to listen to such impieties, though the heretics should threaten us with a thousand deaths."

Also in Alexandria was a young deacon named Athanasius. Almost fifty years younger than Arius, Athanasius was a tireless opponent of Arius. Athanasius insisted that Jesus is God-with-us, true God become truly human. He insisted that Jesus, the Son of God, has always existed. The Son of God is not a created being. Certainly, the birth of Jesus in a Bethlehem cattle shed occurred at a specific time in a specific place. But before that birth the Son of God existed in fellowship with God the Father. The divine person called in Scripture the Word of God or the Son of God or the Wisdom of God became human, yet this divine person has always existed, according to Athanasius.

The struggle between the party of Arius and the party of Athanasius waged fiercely for almost sixty years. From about 320 to 380 C.E., the tug-of-war between the two groups made the final outcome uncertain. Sometimes the Arian party gained power. When that happened, Athanasius was exiled from Alexandria, forced to flee for his life. When the Athanasian party gained power, Athanasius was called back. No less than five times he was banished and recalled. It is perhaps hard to imagine how heated the controversy between the Arians and the Athanasians was in the fourth century. In those days, people did not dismiss doctrine as unimportant and bothersome. Many common people had a passionate opinion on these matters. A historian of the time reports that the "butcher and baker" argued about whether Jesus is *truly* God or only *like* God. Philip Butin recounts how the opinions of Arius were spread by means of popular songs and quips. "At the height of the controversy, people are reported to have gone about in the streets of Alexandria shouting 'There was when he was not' in Greek, a quote that summarized how Arius's view of Christ differed from the orthodox view."[2]

In 325 C.E., the emperor Constantine, tired of the controversy, called together a conference of bishops, about two hundred in all, to settle the question. The conference was held in Nicaea, a seaside town in northwest Turkey. This conference produced a first version of the Nicene Creed, written in Greek, which decisively rejected Arius.

The view that God created the Son, the second person of the Trinity, at a particular time was rejected. Jesus was affirmed at Nicaea to be eternally preexistent, along with God the Father. The view that Jesus is not fully God, but a junior god, was rejected. Jesus was affirmed at Nicaea to be fully divine, completely one in divine essence with God the Father. The Nicene Creed is a clear guideline for Christian thinking about Jesus. Jesus is fully and truly God. Nothing less.

[2] See Butin, *The Trinity,* 24 n. 40.

The Nicene Council in 325 did not settle the argument among Christian thinkers around the Mediterranean basin. Constantine's hope that his council would calm the choppy waters of church relations was dashed. Yet, the Nicene Creed did set the lines of future discussion. It survived the five banishments of Athanasius and has lasted to the present day as a basic framework for understanding who Jesus Christ is.[3]

The Shocking Claim That Jesus Is Human

If the Council of Nicaea set in place one important plank in the platform of belief in Jesus Christ, another crucial plank was added one hundred years later. Central to Christian faith is the belief in Jesus as fully divine, truly God. But equally important is the conviction that Jesus Christ is fully human, truly a person.

Christians have sometimes fenced in Jesus' humanity, restricting it. Jesus cannot really be truly human, they think. Surely Jesus did not ever have to learn anything. Surely Jesus never felt frustrated or angry. Surely Jesus did not ever feel lonely or fearful. The result of this view is a Jesus who does not look very human at all. Some believers, for example, assume that the infant Jesus had a complete awareness of his identity as the Savior of the world, that the toddler Jesus knew he was the second person of the Trinity incarnate, that the young child Jesus knew he was to suffer and die and be raised on the third day. This assumption comes from a deep and full well, the well of faith in Jesus Christ and a sturdy insistence on the full divinity of Jesus. But the deep well of faith must also insist on the full humanity of Jesus.

In his book *The Good News from North Haven,* Michael Lindvall tells the story of the annual Christmas pageant of the fictional Second Presbyterian Church in North Haven. The story illustrates this deep resistance to Jesus' full humanity, a resistance that, in this story, takes a poignant, even comic form. For forty-seven years, Alvina Johnson had directed the pageant, producing a long line of predictable, identical performances. But this year, the pageant was

---

[3] See the Appendix for the text of the Nicene Creed.

different. Several young mothers were directing the pageant, and they were determined to introduce some fresh concepts.

During the final rehearsal, the children playing the roles of Mary and Joseph had walked down the center aisle to the familiar lines from the King James Bible, "And Joseph also went up from Galilee, out of the city of Nazareth, into Judea, unto the city of David, which is called Bethlehem . . . to be taxed with Mary his espoused wife, being great with child." But one final innovation was introduced at the last moment. The young mothers had noted that none of the children could much understand King James English, so they changed the narrator's part to the Good News translation of the Bible (Today's English Version). Pleased with their more updated version, they asked each other, "What kid knows what 'great with child' means?"

Michael Lindvall's story continues: "The Good News translation is much more direct at this point. So, as Mary and Joseph entered, the Narrator read, 'Joseph went to register with Mary who was promised in marriage to him. She was pregnant.'

"As that last word echoed from the Narrator through the PA system into the full church, our little Joseph, hearing it, froze in his tracks, gave Mary an incredulous look, peered out at the congregation, and said, 'Pregnant? What do you mean, pregnant?' This, of course, brought down the house. My wife, wiping tears from her eyes, leaned over to me and said, 'You know, that may well be just what Joseph actually said.' "[4]

At that moment, the young Joseph in the pageant was hit with the reality of the full humanity of Jesus. Mary was *pregnant*—with *Jesus?* This is a shocker. God became flesh in a dimly lit barn through an ordinary birth. The Son of God born to a young, unwed mother. The Word of God with an umbilical cord. Some Christians would rather think about Jesus as King of kings, Lord of lords, with the flashing sword of victory held high in his hand. But remembering the vulnerable ordinariness of Jesus' birth is as important to Christian understandings about Jesus as his glorious

---

[4] Michael Lindvall, *The Good News from North Haven* (New York: Doubleday, 1991), 14–15.

divine origin. Jesus' complete humanness is as important as his complete divinity.

If Jesus is fully God and fully human, this must mean that Jesus has two natures, one divine and one human. Every other person that has ever lived has just one nature—a human nature. Each human person is, well, a *human* person. Jesus is the only person who is *both* a human person and the eternal Son of God. Although this kind of double-talk about Jesus is difficult to comprehend, both affirmations are crucially important. If Jesus isn't really completely God, then he cannot be our Lord and Savior. If Jesus isn't really completely human, then God is not truly with us and for us.

The instinct of the early church that Jesus Christ has two natures—divine and human—arose not out of the dusty archives of a monastery library, but out of the worshiping life of the community. The early church was convinced that any other way of expressing the identity of Jesus would be inadequate. Jesus Christ is worshiped and glorified in prayer, hymn, preaching, and service; he is divine. Jesus Christ was a person, just like us except for sin, and knows all our sorrows; he is human.

The Council of Chalcedon was convened in 451 to put into words this core conviction of Jesus' full divinity and full humanity. Like the Council of Nicaea one hundred and twenty-five years earlier, the firecrackers of argument fizzled and cracked at every turn. Some Christian thinkers in the fifth century thought that the best way to think of Jesus is as "God become human." This idea *tended* to stress the divinity of Jesus so much that the humanity was covered up like a mask. Other Christian thinkers thought that the best way to think of Jesus is as a "two-natured person." This idea *tended* to suggest that Jesus had two personalities, somehow coexisting in one body.

These two points of view caused vigorous controversy. They seemed irreconcilable. But at the Council of Chalcedon, over five hundred bishops gathered together to try to put into words the Christian conviction that Jesus Christ is truly God-with-us and truly one-of-us. The council appointed a committee, giving them the daunting task of writing up a statement. The committee's work is a document, written in Greek, called the Chalcedonian Definition. The definition begins by saying, "Following, then, the holy fathers, we unite in teaching all people to confess the one and only Son, our Lord Jesus Christ." It then affirms that Jesus "is perfect both in deity and also in humanness," that he is "actually God and actually human." To emphasize the point, it repeats that Jesus "is of the same reality as God as far as his deity is concerned and of the same reality as we are ourselves as far as his humanness is concerned," adding a crucial disclaimer: "sin only excepted."

Then the definition tries to explain how this can be. The two natures, divine and human, "are not nullified by the union." They are not mixed together, like hydrogen and oxygen to form a third thing, water. Each nature is still a nature, divine or human, but they are "together the one and only and only-begotten Logos of God, the Lord Jesus Christ."

The Council of Chalcedon bumped up against the limits of human language—Greek, Latin, English, or any other language—in expressing the reality of Jesus Christ. Instead of trying to explain how this is all *possible,* the council bishops simply stated their best understanding of the truth of the faith, affirmed the earlier work of the Nicene Creed, and reminded the church that, fundamentally, they were called to confess the name of the Lord, Jesus Christ.

The Chalcedonian Definition has, like the Nicene Creed, stood the test of time. It continues to serve as a basic structure for Christian belief. At times in the history of the church the full humanity of Jesus has been forgotten. At other times, the full divinity of Jesus is muted. The definition, even in its dense, compact, complex language is a guideline for the church today to express its faith in this particular time and place.

In these days, though, the Chalcedonian Definition is frequently criticized as incoherent and completely inadequate for modern Christians, and that it makes no sense psychologically. Nobody can have two natures, people point out, except perhaps someone with multiple personality disorder. Furthermore, it is dated in its concepts and categories. The language of the Nicene

Creed and the Chalcedonian Definition use words that creak with age. Words like "essence" and "nature" and "substance" are old Greek philosophical terms, not modern concepts. We should relegate these ancient documents to a museum, or even a dustbin, so the argument goes.

Other people are disillusioned with the whole notion of ancient creeds and confessions that guide our faith and life today. They see that the process of formulating these ancient statements of faith, like the Nicene Creed and the Chalcedonian Definition, were marked by distressing displays of very un-Christlike behavior. Bishops and popes and emperors buzzed around issues of faith like fierce wasps. Giant personalities and egos were involved. Politics played a role. Geography played a role. Careers were destroyed and careers were established. Furious exchanges of letters flew from Rome to Alexandria to Constantinople. One historian of the time said, with a hint of exasperation, that "the highways were filled with galloping bishops." Must our faith be shaped by such imperfect people?

The answer is yes. God has always used deeply flawed people. The Bible tells the stories of some of them. The failings of Noah, Abraham, Jacob, Moses, and David in the Old Testament include adultery, murder, lying, betrayal, and all sorts of violence. The New Testament continues the saga of sinful people through whom God's purposes still get done. The history of believing people is the history of greedy, selfish, power-hungry, stubborn people. It is also the history of committed and faithful people, seized by the grace of God and filled with passion for the truth of God. Frequently, of course, these contradictory characteristics jostle for space in the same people.

The ancient statements of faith that continue to guide Christian doctrine today were written by people marked by all the failings so familiar to each of us. But this does not require us to turn away from them. Instead of elbowing ancient doctrinal documents out of the way, Christians ought to include them in their own top drawer of valuables of the faith. The great strength of both Nicaea and Chalcedon is their affirmations of the Christian confession that Jesus is Lord.

The Extravagant Claim That God Accepts Us

It is not always easy to receive a gift. The natural, "Oh, wow!" of children grows up to adult murmurs of "Oh, you shouldn't have." This happens even with God's gifts to us. Many believers find it hard to receive gladly God's generous gift of grace in Jesus Christ. Again and again, the church has needed the clear call to accept the love of God as a gift to be received, not earned, bought, bartered, or hoarded.

The sixteenth century was one such time when the church needed this reminder. What happened then is often called the Reformation, but could more accurately be called the *reformations*. England, Scotland, the Netherlands, Switzerland, France, Germany, Italy, Czechoslovakia, Poland, and Hungary all experienced their own forms of the Reformation. Yet, despite the rich diversity of events, personalities, and influences, two names stand out above all others. Martin Luther and John Calvin were as different as can be imagined in temperament. Luther was German; Calvin, French. Luther was bold and earthy, with a hearty appetite and a hearty laugh. Calvin was frail, pale, and frequently ill. Luther is considered the founder of the Lutheran tradition and Calvin of the Reformed tradition. But, theologically, they agreed on almost everything. In fact, the theological differences between the Lutheran tradition and the Reformed tradition are probably less significant, to the untrained eye, than the differences between a lesser yellowlegs sandpiper and a greater yellowlegs sandpiper. Just as birdwatchers love to catalog small differences among birds, theologians have often highlighted the small differences among theological traditions.

One important thing Luther and Calvin agreed on is the doctrine of justification. The story is told that Martin Luther, an Augustinian monk, was plagued with strong feelings of worthlessness and anxiety. He wrote, "I was a good monk, and I kept the rule of my order so strictly that I may say that if ever a monk got to heaven by his monkery, it was I."[5] Yet, Luther did not feel that he deserved salvation and did not feel confident in the love and grace of God.

---

[5] Roland Bainton, *Here I Stand* (New York: Abingdon-Cokesbury Press, 1950), 65.

A breakthrough occurred one day when Luther was reading in the Bible Paul's letter to the Romans. There he read about the righteousness of God. He had always assumed that this meant God's justice and judgment against sin. But he suddenly realized that the righteousness of God means that God gives to us righteousness, a righteousness that comes through Jesus Christ. He saw that we are saved by the grace of God in Jesus Christ, not through a perfect following of the law or our own good works.

This is the doctrine of justification. Luther reported later that his discovery of this theme—the grace of God through Jesus Christ is all that is required—was like a "gate to heaven" for him. Calvin agreed. He said that justification is "the main hinge on which religion turns." If Luther and Calvin are right, justification sounds like a claim of enormous significance and transforming effect. Yet, justification is a theological word that produces yawns and sighs for most Christians today. It seems to have sedative power rather than the power to make our hearts sing and our spirits soar.

Justification is a doctrine that states one simple and utterly basic truth: in Jesus Christ we are accepted. Acceptance is a deep yearning of all people. Children long to be accepted by their classmates and friends. Adolescents yearn for acceptance; they will do almost anything to get it. Adults, too, make crucial choices that are tinged by the striving to belong.

It is part of human nature to want to belong, to be taken in and accepted. After all, accepted people thrive and flourish. Longing for complete acceptance is a good and healthy thing.

The alternative to acceptance is deep psychic pain. Ernest Becker remarked in his book *The Denial of Death,* "Hell, then, is the state of not being accepted. In hell, no one takes an interest in you."[6] Justification doctrine affirms, quite simply, that God takes an interest in you. In his classic book *Institutes of the Christian Religion,* John Calvin defines justification "simply as the acceptance with which God receives us into his favor."[7] God does not first check off a long list of requirements in order for us to win or

---

[6] Ernest Becker, *The Denial of Death* (New York: Free Press, 1973), 106.
[7] John Calvin, *Institutes of the Christian Religion,* ed. John T. McNeill, trans. Ford Lewis Battles (Philadelphia: Westminster Press, 1960), 3.11.2.

earn acceptance. God loves unconditionally. The price tag for God's acceptance is nothing. It's free. Theologian Gerhard Forde says, "The gospel of justification by faith is such a shocker, such an explosion, because it is an absolutely unconditional promise."[8] Oddly, though, absolutely free and unconditional grace is hard to swallow. It goes so deeply against the grain of how life works. We expect that our good deeds will be rewarded and our bad deeds will be punished. There must be some sort of cosmic accounting. This is just the way it goes. The free grace of God in Jesus Christ—no strings attached—just cannot be true. There must be a catch. Robert Farrar Capon remarks that "The human race, faced with the choice between a gift and a deal, will almost invariably prefer the deal."[9]

When the free acceptance of God does dawn on the dark night of despair, transformation occurs. A story of God's complete acceptance is told in the book *Racehoss, Big Emma's Boy,* by Albert Race Sample. Racehoss grew up in a violent home and was a repeat offender in the Texas prison system. The familiar cycle emerged: prison, parole, offense, prison. Racehoss learned survival skills in an environment of brutality almost beyond comprehension. But one day, in the darkness of solitary confinement, he experienced God's acceptance, even of him who had been rejected by family and society. The author tells the story,

> The slamming of the two steel doors still rang in my ears. Sitting naked on the slab in pitch-black silence, I hung my head as the tears bounded off the floor onto my feet. . . . Sweat poured. Gritting my teeth, I hugged and rocked myself, trying to squeeze back the consuming fear. . . . I pounded my knuckles and banged my head against the unyielding concrete. . . . I mauled myself, scratching and tearing my body. Slumped, exhausted, on the slab, I covered my face with both hands and cried out, "Help me, God!! Help meee!!. . ."
>
> A ray of light between my fingers. Slowly uncovering my face, the whole cell was illuminated like a 40-watt bulb was

[8] Gerhard Forde, *Justification by Faith: A Matter of Life and Death* (Philadelphia: Fortress Press, 1982), 24.

[9] Robert Farrar Capon, *The Fingerprints of God: Tracking the Divine Suspect through a History of Images* (Grand Rapids: Wm. B. Eerdmans Publishing Co., 2000), 55.

turned on. The soft light soothed and I no longer was afraid.
Engulfed by a presence, I felt it reassuring me. No pressure any
more, I breathed freely. I had never felt such well being, so
good, in all my life. Safe. Loved. . . .
    And the voice within talked through the pit of my belly,
"Don'cha worry about a thing. But you must tell them about
me."
    I lay back on the slab. A change had taken place. Never
before had I felt so totally loved. That's really all I ever wanted.
The biggest need in my life fulfilled in an instant. And I loved
that Presence back.[10]

Racehoss's conversion had only begun. But the sheer intrusion
of God's grace into that hellhole is a vivid picture of justification.

The doctrine of justification should have been an affirmation of
the Christian faith for all believers from diverse traditions. Yet, it
became the occasion of argument for many centuries. Catholics
assumed that the Protestants were proposing a religion that dismissed laws, morals, and religious duties. They thought justification doctrine in the hands of people like Luther and Calvin looked
a lot like a blank check—you can do anything you want, what you
do doesn't matter. Protestants supposed that the Catholics were
more interested in salvation through the church than salvation
through Jesus Christ. They thought that justification in the hands
of the Catholic hierarchy looked a lot like an "overdue notice" in
the mail—you had to pay up, interest included, in order to get
salvation.

This suspicion between Catholics and Protestants has endured
for more than four hundred years, but there has been encouraging
improvement in recent decades on coming to agreement on important matters of the faith. In 1999, Lutherans and Catholics produced
a document that states broad areas of common belief on justification. The document states that "as sinners our new life is solely due
to the forgiving and renewing mercy that God imparts as a gift and
we receive in faith, and never can merit in any way." It goes on to
explain the background of this statement of justification:

[10] Albert Race Sample, *Racehoss: Big Emma's Boy* (New York: Ballantine Books,
1986), 276–77.

In faith, we together hold the conviction that justification is the work of the triune God. The Father sent his Son into the world to save sinners. The foundation and presupposition of justification is the incarnation, death, and resurrection of Christ. Justification thus means that Christ himself is our righteousness, in which we share through the Holy Spirit in accord with the will of the Father. Together we confess: By grace alone, in faith in Christ's saving work and not because of any merit on our part, we are accepted by God and receive the Holy Spirit, who renews our hearts while equipping and calling us to good works.[11]

This compact statement makes several absolutely fundamental claims. First, we all need help. We cannot mend our own brokenness. Second, the triune God wills to rescue us, to save us from the consequences of our alienation from God. Third, Christ is the one who accomplishes this rescue, this salvation. Fourth, the Holy Spirit makes us new people and calls us to live a life fitting for new people. In short: it is by grace that we are saved, and it is through faith that we receive this grace.

For many Christian believers, perhaps these fundamental claims seem old, settled, even obvious. But for the person who gives up the futile effort to earn God's love, the gospel is brand new. For the person who realizes for the first time that God forgives sins, puts them away, and does not look back, the gospel is brand new. For those persons who finally see that the mercy of God is expansive enough even for them, the gospel is brand new. Far from being a creaky, dusty old doctrine, justification is the very heart of the gospel.

The New Clay Pots: Global Christian Communities

Kincaid Chance, the young narrator of David James Duncan's book that we looked at earlier, *The Brothers K,* puzzles over the question of who Jesus is.

---

[11] Joint Declaration on the Doctrine of Justification (Grand Rapids: Wm. B. Eerdmans Publishing Co., 2000), 15.

Personally I'm not sure just who or what Christ is. I still pray to
Him in a pinch, but I talk to myself in a pinch too—and I'm get-
ting less and less sure there's difference. . . . Mamma tries to
clear up all the confusion by saying that Christ is exactly what
the Bible says He is. But what *does* the Bible say He is? On one
page He's a Word, on the next a bridegroom, then He's a boy,
then a scapegoat, then a thief in the night; read on and He's the
messiah, then oops, He's a rabbi, and then a fraction—a third of
a Trinity—then a fisherman, then a broken loaf of bread. I guess
even God, when He's human, has trouble deciding just what
He is.[12]

Kincaid's bewilderment has been shared by many, from Jesus'
time with his disciples around Galilee to today, when claims about
Jesus veer wildly from one side to another. There has been no single way of understanding Jesus. Right from the beginning, in the
New Testament, there is variety. The Jesus of Mark's Gospel—a
Jesus who sleeps through a thunderstorm, a Jesus who is sometimes tired and frustrated—is quite different from the Jesus of the
book of Revelation—the Lamb who was slain but raised to glorious majesty and power. The Jesus of the church's doctrinal tradition, complete with complex, philosophically precise definitions,
is quite different from the Jesus of the great mystical writers, who
included in their prayers to Jesus as mother and Jesus as bride
among their prayers.

And now, theological conversation has become global. No
longer is the theological scene monopolized by Europeans and
North Americans. Africans, Asians, and South Americans, for
example, are contributing rich theological language to the conversation. Women and other peoples long silenced are speaking up.
The truth of the gospel is being expressed in the many particular
images and understandings of many particular people.

African Christians, for example, are as deeply influenced by
their own cultural ways of thinking as the Nicaean Council bishops were influenced by theirs. African theologians are suggesting
uniquely African titles for Jesus Christ, seeking to link Christian

---

[12] David James Duncan, *The Brothers K* (New York: Bantam Books, 1996), 61.

faith in Jesus with the long traditions of the African peoples. One African title for Jesus is "Victor." The powers of the spirits, Africans know, are often negative powers, threatening the physical and mental health of people. Jesus fights against the powers of the evil spirits and is victorious over them.

Another uniquely African title for Jesus is "Ancestor." This title indicates that Jesus is respected and beloved, honored for his wisdom. He is one with us but has gone before us and leads the way. Echoes of traditional Christology, with language of "fully human and fully divine," can be heard in ancestor language. The affirmations are deeply biblical—that Jesus Christ is God-with-us, the Lord who has walked the human walk and is now our Ancestor, the One who summons us to the day when we will all be united with him.

Related to this title is another one, "Elder Brother." In traditional African societies, the elder brother takes the role of teacher and leader. For African Christians, Jesus is their elder brother. Other traditional African titles are more ambiguous. Some have suggested "Chief" as an African title for Jesus. But others conclude that this is a title with distant and remote connotations. The chief of a village can often be judgmental, not gracious, often aloof, not present. African Christians bring their own particular cultural resources to worship, seeking both to be faithful to God revealed in Jesus Christ and respectful of their own cultural traditions.

Asian Christians, as well, are voicing their faith in Jesus in fresh ways that are particular to their culture. Of course, there is no such thing as "Asian culture"—just as there is no such thing as "African culture" or "European culture," either. There are hundreds of distinct cultures on each continent. Koreans, Filipinos, Japanese, Chinese all contribute unique voices to the global theological conversation. Jesus the Liberator, Jesus the Shaman or Healer, and Jesus the Worker are some titles of Christ that are discussed in Asian contexts.

One of the liveliest centers of conversation in global Christian theology is among women. The oppression and suffering of women in the world is widespread. Much of this oppression is firmly entrenched in the patterns of cultures and the structures of society. In spite of decades of vigorous advocacy for women around the world, abuses of women's bodies and spirits continue. For Christians, the challenge is acute. How can the gospel be good news for women who are systematically marginalized? How can Jesus help young girls who are sold or traded? How can the church be a beacon of hope for women who are not valued as fully human? Women and men committed to the flourishing of women and other oppressed peoples feel compelled to respond to these old, deep patterns in society at many levels. They engage in political activity. They serve as educators, medical professionals, agriculturalists, anthropologists, pastors, and fund-raisers. They also find comfort and strength in the language of faith. Reclaiming old medieval images of Jesus as mother, discovering courage in the prophets of the Bible, finding a community of support and encouragement with other Christians—in these ways, women are speaking their faith in their own voice.

The current conversations about Jesus by women, Africans, Asians, Hispanics, and many others have sometimes challenged traditional and classical Christian theology, at times in strident tones of anger and pain. Settled and secure believers feel criticized and blamed. Yet, if we can learn to listen to one another in a spirit of openness and hospitality, these contemporary voices help expand our understanding of God's grace in Jesus Christ. They motivate us to join Jesus in alleviating the sufferings of the world. They enrich our worship of God. For these reasons, Christian theology must be open to a wide diversity of voices, resisting the impulse to take cover or comfort in familiar language. The Holy Spirit poured out new languages on the startled disciples on Pentecost morning. The Spirit is still pouring out new languages for faith in the global conversation today.

4

Cleansing or Victory or Ransom: How Are We Saved? (Part 1)

*M*ajor media executives in North America know that people are interested in Jesus. They produce made-for-television miniseries about Jesus to be aired during Easter week. Sleek and tanned actors play the parts of Jesus, the disciples, and Mary Magdalene. National magazines put Jesus on their covers at Christmas and Easter. But all this interest spills out into very different streams. Some people consider Jesus to be an inspiration for their lives. A model teacher and listener. A sage. Other people regard Jesus as the founder of the Christian religion. They are intrigued with him in the same fashion that they are intrigued with Muhammad, Buddha, or founders of other religions.

Christians, too, are interested in learning about the wide variety of world religions and the impressive virtues of religious leaders. But faith in Jesus as the Christ, the Savior of the world, goes much farther than warm regard. Christians believe that Jesus has saved the world from sin, saved people from the dark isolation chambers of greed, pride, self-hatred, and envy, saved people for authentic lives of worship and service. Christians believe that the gospel of Jesus Christ is good news. The best news possible. Christians believe that, because of Jesus, the world will be led through all the sufferings and injustices that now convulse the world into a peace and harmony that is God's unwavering will for all people.

Furthermore, Christians believe that salvation, all the good things God intends for the world, happens through a death, the death of Jesus on the cross. God reveals God's love and mercy in the death of Jesus. In that death, all that has gone wrong in life is taken up into the heart of God and overcome. By means of that death, the world is saved. Such a statement can hardly be spoken before the questions burst out: But *how* does this happen? How can a death be saving? Why did Jesus have to die? What sense can all this make?

Fredricka Matthews-Green, a Christian writer, received an e-mail from a friend who was struggling with the question of how it is that Jesus died for our sins.[1] The friend briefly summarized his life in his note. Raised in a nominally Jewish home, he moved first to atheism and then to nontheistic Eastern religion before he came to consider the Christian faith. He wanted to believe the claims of the Christian faith, but it just didn't make much sense to him. He wrote: "How could the Father send the Son, if they are one? How could God the Son die? Why was it necessary that his body be resurrected? Please don't take this as being argumentative; I would really like to find some way to understand. As much as I love Jesus' teaching and person, no matter how I turn it around in my mind, no matter how much I read, I cannot understand what it means to say that Jesus died for our sins."

Matthews-Green answered his e-mail letter graciously and honestly. She wrote, "It seems that what happened (and continues to happen) is that people somehow began to sense that Jesus Christ is still alive and in some inexplicable way present to them; along with this, they find that their burden of sin is lifted, and that this is somehow because of his death on the Cross and Resurrection. Plenty of 'somehows' in that sentence; we're dealing with something inchoate, but nevertheless insistent."

Matthews-Green then makes a helpful comparison in her response to her friend. She remarks that farmers have always known that light makes plants grow. They knew this many millennia before the complicated processes of photosynthesis were discovered by scientists. Similarly, even though Christians struggle and stammer to give precise explanations of how salvation works through Jesus' death, they still know it. Somehow.

---

[1] From the personal correspondence of Professor Stan Rock. Used with permission.

C. S. Lewis once described this "somehow" of Christian accounts of salvation. He said, "The central Christian belief is that Christ's death has somehow put us right with God and given us a fresh start. Theories as to how it did this are another matter. A good many different theories have been held as to how it works; what all Christians are agreed on is that it does work."[2]

Biblical Accounts of Salvation

The New Testament was written by followers of Jesus. They were not disinterested bystanders. They had been changed forever by the grace of God, and they were eager to share the good news with others. The New Testament is a rich mine of testimony to the experience and reality of salvation through Jesus Christ. Just as Scripture is the primary source for learning about the life of Jesus, so it is the primary source for understanding salvation through Jesus.

Some biblical images of salvation were spoken by Jesus himself. In Matthew 20:28 Jesus said to his disciples, who were arguing about which of them was the greatest, "The Son of Man came not to be served but to serve, and to give his life a ransom for many." Here, Jesus sees that he must die. He also sees that his death will liberate people, will mark a point of transformation for them. Although the Garden of Gethsemane prayer signaled Jesus' anguish about his impending suffering and death, he faithfully and obediently accepted his death as a unique call from his Father in heaven.

He tried to explain this to his disciples. Jesus said, "The Son of Man is to be betrayed into human hands, and they will kill him, and three days after being killed, he will rise again" (Mark 9:31). The Gospel accounts clearly show us that Jesus knew about his death and knew, as well, the meaning of his death. Eugene Peterson asks pointedly, "What exactly did Jesus do? Our gospel witnesses make it clear that his death was no accidental miscarriage of Roman justice, no cruel Greek tragic fate that inexorably overtook him."[3]

---

[2] C. S. Lewis, *Mere Christianity* (New York: Macmillan Co., 1952), 57.
[3] Eugene Peterson, "The Play of Salvation," *Perspectives,* August/September 2000, 9.

This does not mean, of course, that the rigged trial and public execution of Jesus was right and just. Far from it. Putting Jesus to death was a crime. It was a tragedy. But these conclusions are not the final word. They are based only on an ordinary, human way of evaluating a historical event. Christians have the additional insight of faith, which gives them the confidence to say, "Jesus was crucified for the salvation of the world. What was a blatant act of injustice is, by the grace of God, the source of the world's restoration and hope." It is this core conviction that Christian believers have expressed, in a variety of ways, for more than two thousand years.

The apostle Paul, writing twenty years or so after Jesus' resurrection, attempted to explain in a number of ways the way salvation works. He said, "[God] made him to be sin who knew no sin, so that in him we might become the righteousness of God" (2 Cor. 5:21). This explanation suggests that Christ exchanged places with us. He became sin so that we might become righteous.

In another place, he said, "I have been crucified with Christ; and it is no longer I who live, but it is Christ who lives in me. And the life I now live in the flesh I live by faith in the Son of God, who loved me and gave himself for me" (Gal. 2:19–20). Here Paul makes some remarkable claims. He says that he has been crucified with Christ. He says that Christ lives in him. He says that his own daily life is made possible because of these two great facts. Paul is making some kind of salvation explanation—that he has been united with Christ in the crucifixion. So close a union is this that Christ lives "in" him, nourishing his faith and his very existence.

Even the closing remarks in Paul's letters to the emerging churches, collected in the New Testament, reveal some hints about how salvation works. At the end of the book of Romans, for example, Paul says, "Welcome one another, therefore, just as Christ has welcomed you, for the glory of God." Paul is instructing the early Christians about much more than social etiquette. He is saying that Christ has *welcomed* us. Salvation, then, is something like hospitality, something like coming home, something like the wide-opened arms of God taking us in.

In Paul's letter to the Ephesians, salvation is explained by using images of restoration, of bringing together those long estranged.

Ephesians 2:13 says that in Jesus Christ we, who were once far away, have been brought near through the blood of Jesus. People long separated and suspicious of one another are brought back together, seated at the same table, once again. People who have been refugees from the love of God, lost and alone, far from their true home are brought back. Salvation is a lot like coming home, like reconciliation, like a fresh start. Peoples are reconciled with peoples. People are reconciled with God. This reconciliation is accomplished through the blood of Jesus. No further explanation is given in this text. The astonishing claim is simply stated, that Jesus' death is what brings together those who were long separated and lost.

In the next verse, Paul gives a mental picture of what reconciliation is like. He says that Christ is our peace because he has broken down the dividing wall of hostility. No longer does a thick wall of hatred, prejudice, and suspicion exist between peoples. Those days are gone. The new era of peace and reconciliation has come.

The writer of the book of Hebrews explained salvation in terms of sacrifice, high priests, and laws. Jesus Christ is the great high priest who offers himself as a sacrifice for the sins of the whole world. Because of this, Christ is the source of eternal salvation for all who obey him. The unknown writer of Hebrews gives one of the most sophisticated and nuanced accounts of salvation. Yet this writer admits, "About this we have much to say that is hard to explain," because they are slow to learn (Heb. 5:11). All Christian believers who have struggled to understand the meaning of the cross of Jesus Christ, how it is that salvation comes through Christ's death, can well understand this frustrated outburst in the book of Hebrews. It *is* hard to explain. We are, we admit, slow to learn.

Many other explanations of the death and resurrection of Jesus appear in the New Testament, often in letters from the apostles to the young churches around the Mediterranean. Galatians 3:13 states that, "Christ redeemed us from the curse of the law." Romans 5:11 paints a broad canvas of what salvation is: "We . . . boast in God through our Lord Jesus Christ, through whom we have now received reconciliation." In Peter's first letter to scattered

Christians in Asia Minor, he used the image of Christ as a physician, "By his wounds you have been healed." This verse (1 Pet. 2:24) clearly echoes similar words in Isaiah 53, a passage of great significance for early Christians in understanding salvation.

Atonement Theories

In the first few centuries of rapid growth and expansion of the Christian community, believers did not draft a set "theory" of how we receive salvation through Jesus' death and resurrection. Instead, a wide range of images and motifs circulated, most of them drawn directly from the Scriptures, both the Old Testament and the New Testament, that collection of Gospels, letters, and other documents that were gradually gathered together and recognized as the Word of God to the church.

The early church never made an official declaration on the precise way that Jesus' death and resurrection guarantees our salvation. It seems that right from the beginning, from the voices of the New Testament itself, the Christian tradition has been open to quite a wide range of approaches to the atonement. There is so much variety on this doctrine of the Christian faith, in fact, that some way of sorting through the possibilities is needed.

The word "atonement" is an invented English word with no roots in either Latin or Greek, the usual path for theological terms. It first appeared in sixteenth-century documents in England as two words—"at onement." A 1599 document, with old English spellings, refers to "the redempcion, reconciliacion, and at onement of mankinde with God the father." Soon, the two words were joined and were used to refer to any sort of agreement or harmony. An early history of Great Britain reported that "after three great and dangerous Battles, [they] came to an atonement." The word atonement, then, really does mean "at-one-ment."

The rich possibilities in the long tradition of Christian reflection are sometimes organized by *atonement theories*. These are attempts to explain the saving significance of Jesus' life, death, and resurrection by focusing on a particular image of how salvation comes through Jesus Christ. For example, one early explanation of salvation suggested that we are saved because Jesus Christ won a great victory on the cross. The crucifixion looks for all the world like a terrible defeat, but in reality it is a decisive victory. The powers of evil are destroyed and Jesus Christ is the victor.

Another early explanation said that Jesus Christ paid a ransom price for us. We are kidnapped by sin and held hostage. Our release is possible only if a great price is paid. Jesus paid that price and we were set free.

Each of these early explanations uses an image, or metaphor. The first uses the image of a military battle, the second the image of a ransom payment. Of course, the cross and empty tomb are not *actually* a military battle or a sack of ransom money. They are particular events that took place in Jerusalem roughly around 30 C.E. But believers have used these images of victory and ransom, as well as others, as a way of comprehending the big Christian claims about Jesus Christ.

The diversity and variety in atonement images throughout the history of Christian theology is a testimony to the continuing effort to understand salvation. Christians have always put their confidence and trust in their Lord and Savior Jesus Christ. A Christian believer in the twenty-first century or the sixteenth century or the fifth century or on Pentecost morning might hesitate if asked, "But how does salvation *work*? How can *death* on a cross give us *life*?" The question might puzzle a believer in each of these times. "How does it *work*?" they might say. "I don't know how it *works!* But I do know that I am saved from my sin and now belong to Jesus! That's all that really matters."

Precise, exact explanations of the "mechanics" of salvation seem to be beyond the ability of human thought. Still, believers make an effort to find the right picture or metaphor to express their confidence in Jesus Christ. In trying to express this reality, Christian believers of various times, places, cultures, and circumstances might explain salvation in quite different ways.

It is important, at this point, to remember that the cross and the empty tomb do not acquire their saving reality by theologians and thoughtful Christian believers. Our brilliant insights or hard thinking about these events is not what conjures up their saving power.

It is the will and act of God that the cross and empty tomb are the means for the reconciliation of the world with God. Christians recognize, confess, and believe this based on the witness of Scripture and the work of the Holy Spirit that confirms it to them. Christians then attempt to express the reconciliation of God and the world through Jesus Christ by drawing out and reflecting on the many ways Scripture itself speaks of this reality. The effort to try to *explain* salvation does not mean that the reality of God's act of grace, mercy, and judgment in Jesus Christ is not real, that somehow it depends on our logic. Rather, it means that the believer, who gratefully counts himself as included in the reach of God's grace, searches for the words to say it, explain it, state it.

Important, hard questions immediately arise when a believer thinks about salvation. Why do we need salvation in the first place? What *is* salvation? How is it that a death can bring salvation? How does forgiveness happen? Why wasn't Jesus' *life* of teaching and healing enough for salvation? Where is Jesus now? These are questions that some Christian believers struggle with in an attempt to understand their faith. Other Christians may only realize the weight of these questions when someone asks them to explain salvation. Then they discover it is not easy to put into words how salvation works and what it means.

Because there are so many different ways to explain salvation, theologians have often developed atonement schemes that attempt to organize all the issues surrounding salvation. One possible scheme organizes various atonement theories according to the predicament, or pressing questions, of each consecutive age in the history of the church. This scheme asks first what the predicament of each particular period of time is and then identifies the Christian understanding of salvation that answers that predicament. Schemes like this one are very general, missing lots of interesting nuances and details, but in a rough way can be helpful.[4]

This chapter, and the next two, will survey a number of important theories, each from a different time in the church's history.

---

[4] Paul Fiddes, *Past Event and Present Salvation* (Louisville, Ky.: Westminster/John Knox Press, 1989); see esp. pp. 3–13.

Each of these theories will specify first what the predicament of humanity is: What is the problem? and then how the death and resurrection of Jesus Christ is understood: How does Jesus Christ solve that problem? Each theory uses a particular metaphor or image to explain salvation. None of these theories can be considered a complete explanation of salvation. The Bible did not content itself with one explanation. Neither are Christian believers required to settle firmly on just one image of salvation.

The Problem of Uncleanness and the Solution of Cleansing

An atonement image that made sense to the New Testament writers has roots that go deep into the religious rituals and customs of the Old Testament. Religious life for the ancient Hebrew people was organized around rituals for purity or holiness. Purity could be lost; it could also be regained. Detailed requirements concerning religious purity are recorded in the Old Testament. Much of the book of Leviticus, for example, is a list of exact requirements for purity. These chapters are strange and foreign to us. We read in Leviticus 11 that weasels, mice, lizards, geckos, crocodiles, and chameleons are all unclean animals. The Hebrew people were instructed not to touch them. If they did happen to touch them, or any dead animal, the requirements for becoming pure or clean once again are spelled out.

Many of the first Christians were Jews, raised and trained according to strict Jewish customs, including the purity rituals. Naturally, the New Testament shows the influence of Jewish thinking on almost every page. For a Jewish believer in Jesus Christ, the problem of humanity could be understood as impurity or uncleanness. If this is the problem, then the corresponding picture of salvation is the cleansing, purifying power of Christ's blood.

The book of Hebrews summarizes how Jesus Christ is the Savior by concluding, "Without the shedding of blood there is no forgiveness of sins" (Heb. 9:22). The writer of Hebrews seems to assume that everyone would naturally agree with this statement. It is stated as something completely self-evident. It is the shedding of blood that washes us clean from our sins.

Another text from the book of Hebrews describes the effects of Jesus' death on those who believe. Believers are encouraged to approach God with "a true heart in full assurance of faith, with our hearts sprinkled clean from an evil conscience and our bodies washed with pure water" (Heb. 10:22). Both hearts and bodies are clean because of Jesus Christ.

This is the picture of salvation that emerges in the old gospel hymn, "There is a fountain filled with blood, drawn from Emmanuel's veins. And sinners, plunged beneath that flood, lose all their guilty stains." People with little or no familiarity with Christian symbolism might be shocked at this song with its blunt images of being washed with blood in order to get clean. They might wonder what kind of weird religion these Christians have. But when this imagery is recognized as an ancient biblical symbol of renewing and cleansing, it becomes more understandable.

The Problem of Evil Powers and the Solution of Victory

Another important atonement image comes from the first few centuries of the church. This was a time when the reality and power of evil forces, the principalities and powers, were vividly experienced by people. It should be emphasized that the power of evil spirits is a widely held belief still today by many cultures in the world. Wise elders in these cultures guide the community through the perils of the spirit world, through rituals, medicines, and incantations. For these communities, the presence of the spirit world is a cultural given, one that shapes their worldview and makes sense of their experience.

North American and European countries, and other countries of the industrial and technological world, have dismissed the notion of evil powers over human beings. Some people consider this a healthy sign of "humanity come of age." Others point out that the modern tendency to deny the reality of anything that cannot be seen, measured, and quantified is actually a naive ignorance of the power and subtlety of evil; such a quick dismissal fails to take seriously the entrenched patterns of evil in hypermodern cultures. The evil powers today might be imagined as systems that trap and crush people. Systems of economic indifference to basic human needs, systems of political oppression, systems of judicial callousness based on money and power, which target certain people for punishment and protect others from prosecution, are the evil powers of affluent, modern societies.

In addition, the easy assumption that there cannot possibly be malignant evil spirits is too blithe and flippant. The wisdom of the Christian tradition has been more sober and serious. In many traditional baptism liturgies, the question is put to the parents of the infant being baptized, or the adult about to be baptized, "Do you renounce the devil?" The answer is, "Yes, I renounce the devil." Here the new Christian is declaring to all the gathered people that she is no longer held by the power of evil, but is now held by the power of love, given to her freely by God in Christ.

Evil powers have a grip on human beings, according to this understanding of salvation, because human beings rebelled against the command of God to obey and serve only God. What freedom humanity once had to worship and serve God joyfully is gone. Salvation, then, is Christ's victory over the powers of evil and the devil. We are saved because the cross is the defeat of the armies of evil, and it is the victory of the army of God. In Scripture, the theme of the defeat of evil is present in 2 Timothy 1:9–10: "This grace was given to us in Christ Jesus before the ages began, but it has now been revealed through the appearing of our Savior Christ Jesus, who abolished death and brought life and immortality to light through the gospel."

Many early theologians explained the cross in terms of victory. The great fourth-century bishop Athanasius, who lived in Alexandria, Egypt, during a time of great controversy in the church, once exclaimed, "So something surprising and startling has happened; for the death, which they thought to inflict as a disgrace, was actually a monument of victory against death itself."[5]

This image of victory occurred not only to early Christians as

[5] Athanasius, "On the Incarnation of the Word," in *Christology of the Later Fathers,* ed. Edward Hardy (Philadelphia: Westminster Press, 1954), 79.

an explanation of salvation. The sixteenth-century reformer Martin Luther preached a sermon on the Apostles' Creed in which he spoke specifically to the children, giving them advice on how to answer questions about their faith. If someone asks you, Luther said, what it means to say that Jesus is Lord, this is what you should say: "I mean by this that I believe that Jesus Christ, the true Son of God, has become my Lord. How? By freeing me from death, sin, hell, and all evil. For before I had no king and lord; the devil was our lord and king; blindness, death, sin, the flesh, and the world were our lords whom we served. Now they have all been driven out and in their stead there has been given to us the Lord Christ, who is the Lord of righteousness, salvation, and all good."[6] Luther also wrote a hymn text that expresses the victory theme. One of the original seven stanzas (as translated by Richard Massie) gives a picture of a cosmic battle.

> It was a strange and dreadful strife
> When life and death contended;
> The victory remained with life,
> The reign of death was ended.
> Holy Scripture plainly saith
> That death is swallowed up by death;
> Its sting is lost forever! Alleluia![7]

The Problem of Kidnap and the Solution of Ransom

Another atonement image from the early church is a variation of the victory motif. It too assumes that humanity is enslaved by the devil. Humanity is caught in a trap that the devil set by tempting human people to sin. The trap was sprung when people willfully rebelled against God. Because of this early disobedience, all the rest of the human race was pulled into the same trap, the same enslavement. However, Jesus is willing, through his death on the cross, to pay the ransom price demanded by the devil—the life of the perfect, obe-

---

[6] Martin Luther, "Sermons on the Catechism," in *Martin Luther: Selections from His Writings,* ed. J. Dillenberger (Garden City, N.Y.: Anchor Books, 1961), 210.
[7] Martin Luther, "Christ Jesus Lay in Death's Strong Bands," in *The Presbyterian Hymnal* (Louisville, Ky.: Westminster/John Knox Press, 1990), no. 110. st. 2.

dient Son of God. In this way, humanity is freed. The late-second-century Christian thinker Irenaeus uses this image when he says that Christ "bound the strong man and set free the weak. . . ." Clearly the devil and all forces of evil are the strong man. We human beings are the weak, unable to break out of our captivity.[8]

This atonement idea is sometimes called the "ransom theory." Jesus pays the ransom price—his own life—and humanity is freed. A hymn text written in the eighteenth century by Samuel Wesley uses the idea of a ransom paid. The third stanza of the hymn, "Behold the Savior of Mankind," contains the line, "'Tis done; The precious ransom's paid."

Sometimes the ransom theme comes linked with a fascinating additional notion. The kidnapping of humanity by the devil is a problem God must solve with cunning and deceit. Satan is not willing to give up humanity and so God offers Jesus to Satan as the bait on a fishhook. Satan sees Jesus and, because his divinity is concealed, Satan assumes Jesus is just another tasty human morsel. Like a fish, Satan goes for the bait. But the hook is Jesus' divinity; this is what sticks in Satan's gullet. Gregory of Nyssa, a fourth-century theologian from Asia Minor, explains, "God . . . veiled himself in our nature. In that way, as it is with greedy fish, Satan might swallow the Godhead like a fishhook along with the flesh, which was the bait."[9]

Because Satan himself becomes trapped on the hook, he must release humanity. Jesus' life is the ransom price paid for humanity's freedom from Satan. A mousetrap is yet another image that appears, sometimes in early and medieval church art. A triptych by Robert Campin, an early-fifteenth-century Dutch painter, pictures the carpenter Joseph, in his workshop, building mousetraps. Here is an illusion to the crucifixion. Jesus is the bait that will trap and crush Satan. The poignancy of the painting is that Jesus' father, Joseph, is unknowingly predicting the death of Jesus by a common task of his trade.

---

[8] Irenaeus, "Against Heresies," 3.19.6, *Ante-Nicene Fathers,* 448.

[9] Gregory of Nyssa, "An Address on Religious Instruction," in *Christology of the Later Fathers,* ed. Edward Hardy (Philadelphia: Westminster Press, 1954), 301.

The Problem of Earthly Bodies and the
Solution of Divinization

Another understanding of salvation assumes that the human predicament has to do with the fact that we are creatures with bodies. Our
bodies prevent our souls from ascending and being united with God.
Our true destiny is for our souls to shake off our mortal bodies and
be united with God. But our bodies pull us down, toward the earth,
toward sin, illness, and death. In this view of who we are as human
beings, salvation happens when Jesus Christ, true God, becomes one
with us. Because Jesus takes on human nature, our human nature is
taken up into his divinity. We can ascend to God in Christ.

One can quickly see how this view of salvation relies on the concepts of the philosophy of Plato, the fourth-century B.C.E. philosopher
who influenced early Christian theology. Plato thought that bodies
hindered the soul from ascent up to the divine. Early Christian theologians, deeply familiar with this concept, used it quite naturally as
a way of understanding salvation. Divinization was the highest goal.
Jesus guarantees this for us by his resurrection and his ascension.

This kind of salvation account has frequently been criticized for
its negative attitude about the material reality of earthly life.
Instead of affirming bodies, the image of divinization considers
bodies to be a major problem for people. Instead of valuing the
stuff of life—birth, babies, children playing in the mud, elderly
people with the wisdom of their years etched on their faces—this
image tends to look beyond all the earthiness that makes up human
life and focus on some distant horizon. This is a fair criticism.

Yet, this image does remind us that there is more to God's purposes for us than meets the eye. God created the earth and pronounced it good. We too must value earthy realities. We must honor
the physical bodies of ourselves and others. We must seek the health
and wholeness of all people. But the early Christian thinkers who
longed for union with God and fellowship in the divine life were
onto something. They remind us that God has even better things
planned for us. When peace is restored to the earth according to
God's will and God's timing, we shall be in the presence of God and
all the angels, not hindered by the cares and aches of this life.

5

Law or Love: How Are We Saved? (Part 2)

*I*f you were a peasant in Europe in the year 1000 C.E., your livelihood would depend on the feudal lord who lived in the large manor house on the hill. Your own house would be a modest hut with no windows and little insulation for the long, cold winters. The lord would own your house and the land you tilled for subsistence crops. You would be forbidden to cut down trees; only the lord had the right to cut and sell trees. You would be allowed only to gather fallen trees for fuel. The shortage of fuel in the winter months would become a bigger and bigger problem every year. You would worry about your children surviving the winter. Four of your eight children would die in their infancy. Cholera and typhoid fever would take the lives of many of your neighbors. Your living children would work beside you in the fields and help tend the animals—not your fields and your animals, but the lord's. You could not read or write, and neither could your children. Life would be filled only with work and worry. There would be no time, and no money, for anything else.

If you were a feudal lord in the year 1000 C.E., your life would be much more secure. However, some of the same realities of disease that your peasants suffer would impact you as well. In addition, even though you would have enough food to eat, it would often be very limited. Seasonal fruits and vegetables, when they were available, would be a treat. Otherwise, tainted meat would often be served up, heavily seasoned with spices to mask the taste and odor. Towns would begin to spring up close to your manor house. There would even be a new inn, which opened its doors to travelers. This would be something new—when you were growing up, only the monasteries served as inns and hostels. You would begin to hear rumors of a crusade to reclaim the Holy Land from the infidels. If the pope called for an army, you would go. It would be your Christian duty, even though you would be worried about your children and their mother being left behind to tend to such a large estate.

The Problem of Offended Honor
and the Solution of Satisfaction

Society was divided up into rigid hierarchies in the year 1000 C.E. The feudal lords assumed their lot in life was to rule. The peasants knew they had no choice but to serve. It was in this setting that the influential Anselm, the archbishop of Canterbury, developed his famous atonement theory. Anselm was, by all accounts, a gentle man with a deep love for God. His devotional writings, prayers, letters, and scholarly treatises all arose from his desire to contemplate and worship God. In his famous treatise, *Why God Became Man,* written at the very end of the eleventh century, Anselm reports that he has received "many earnest requests"[1] to write an answer to the questions: *Why* did God become human and how did Christ's death bring salvation to the world? Why was this all necessary? Could salvation have been achieved another way?

Anselm writes the treatise as a dialogue, a conversation between himself and his friend Boso. They puzzle through some of the most difficult issues in atonement theology. For example, they struggle over the problem of God the Father allowing his well-loved son, Jesus Christ, to suffer and die. What does this say about God? What sort of father is this? Boso is the one to raise this objection:

> **Boso:**   The fact that God allowed Jesus to be treated like this does not seem right for this Divine Father, even though the Son was willing to take up this saving task.

---

[1] Anselm, "Why God Became Man," in *A Scholastic Miscellany: Anselm to Ockham,* ed. Eugene R. Fairweather (Philadelphia: Westminster Press, 1956), 101.

Anselm: On the contrary, it *is* right for the Father to permit the Son to do what the Son most firmly wills to do. After all, the Son wishes both to honor God and to save humanity. The only way was through the sufferings and death of the Son. This he willingly took up.[2]

Not satisfied with this explanation, however, Boso and Anselm want to understand why the only way for salvation was through the sufferings and death of the Son, Jesus Christ. They start with the predicament of human beings. The problem is that people have offended God's honor. After all, God created people and commanded them to obey the divine law. When people did not obey God, this was an affront to God's honor. It was an insult. The balance and harmony and order of the universe was thrown off. Something had to be done in order to right the balance, to restore the order, to bring to God the honor that was properly due.

It is important to remind ourselves that Anselm wrote his treatise *Why God Became Man* at a time of feudal law and codes of honor. Society was structured in such a way that the feudal lords and landowners demanded from their serfs appropriate honor. If that honor was violated—if a serf stole a cow or shot a deer in the lord's forest or did not pay the full amount of the crop tax, the honor of the feudal lord was damaged. In order to restore the lord's honor, the serf was required to make a payment or endure a punishment.

Anselm said that because God is a just God, the dishonoring of God by human sin cannot be overlooked. God cannot turn a blind eye to human sin. Justice requires either punishment for sin or a satisfaction for the offended honor. Punishment would require death for sinners. But God, in great mercy, does not will to destroy all humanity. Instead, God seeks a way to restore the balance of divine honor by the alternative of satisfaction of divine honor.

In the conversation between Anselm and Boso, an immediate problem arises. Human beings are the ones who dishonored God,

---

[2] This, and subsequent sections of Anselm's dialogue, is my paraphrase from Anselm's "Why God Became Man," 100–183.

so human beings are the ones who should give God appropriate satisfaction for that dishonor. But here's where human ability completely fails. Human beings cannot possibly satisfy God's honor. Human sin is vast. Even a tiny, small sin is too big for a person to make right before the holy God.

Anselm and Boso try to work this out:

> **Anselm:** Tell me, then, what will you pay to God for your sin?
>
> **Boso:** Repentance, a contrite and humble heart, fastings and all sorts of bodily labors, mercy in giving and forgiving, and obedience. . . .
>
> **Anselm:** You cannot count this as part of the debt you owe for sin. Those things you naturally owe to God, they are not extras that will satisfy for your debt. . . . What, then, will you pay to God for your sin?
>
> **Boso:** If I owe God myself and all that I can do . . . then I have nothing to repay God for my sin.
>
> **Anselm:** Then what will become of you? How are you going to be saved?

This is the dilemma of sinful humanity—how are we going to be saved?

Anselm and Boso then turn their attention to how it might be possible for this great debt of sin, this great dishonor to God, to be solved. The debt is so enormous, they note, that the satisfaction must be bigger than everything that exists. An infinitely great payment is required.

> **Anselm:** Someone must pay to God for human sin something greater than everything that exists.
>
> **Boso:** I agree.
>
> **Anselm:** But there is nothing that is greater than everything that exists, except God.

Boso: That's right.

Anselm: But no one ought to make this satisfaction except humanity; they are the ones that owe it.

Boso: That seems right.

Anselm: So, because only humanity *ought* to make this satisfaction, but no one but God *can* make it, it is necessary for a God-Man to make it.

Boso: Blessed be God! We have already found out one great truth. Go on, then, for I hope that God will help us.

The only possible way for humanity to be saved is for Jesus Christ, fully God and fully human, to offer his life as a gift of infinite value to the offended honor of God. Jesus *can* render satisfaction because his life is of infinite worth. Jesus substituted for our place. Satisfaction for sin is accomplished. We were the ones who should have made payment for God's offended honor. But Jesus is the one who did it and order is restored.

There is one more interesting piece to Anselm's theory of the atonement, which is often overlooked in descriptions of his account. Because the life of Jesus Christ was of such great value, it deserves a reward from God. Jesus gave a gift of infinite value. This satisfies God's honor, but there is an enormous "surplus." The gift is so large that it is only right that God reward Jesus. But what could Jesus possibly need? Being fully divine, he lacks for nothing. So in gracious generosity, Jesus transfers to humanity the surplus that he earned. He gives them the promise of eternal life and fellowship with God.

Anselm explains, "What greater mercy could be imagined, than for God the Father to say to the sinner, 'Receive my only-begotton Son, and give him for yourself,' and for the Son to say, 'Take me, and redeem yourself'?"

The influence of Anselm's theory of the atonement can hardly be overstated. Much of both Catholic and Protestant atonement theology can trace its roots back to Anselm. Hymns and gospel songs often reflect Anselmian images. Anselm's ideas, or versions of them, have filtered into the consciousness of many believers. If asked what salvation is, many people would respond by saying something like, "Jesus died for my sins. He took my place and paid the price I owed." This kind of explanation is a version of what Anselm wrote more than one thousand years ago.

Anselm's atonement theory has had a rough time lately. Many critics point out the mechanical feel of his account. It portrays God as a litigant in a grudge lawsuit, who requires compensatory damages for lost honor. It suggests that forgiveness is like math—it has to all add up. It suggests that God is motivated by a desire to fill up the divine honor, which is down a quart due to human rebellion. It focuses so much on Jesus' death on the cross that his life of ministry, teaching, and healing is passed over. The resurrection, as well, seems an unnecessary appendix to the drama of salvation.

Anselm's theory also does not account for problems of social disorder and big systemic sins. Salvation seems to occur outside of history or above history, rather than in the actual mess and muck of history. The classic Christian doctrine of the incarnation emphasizes that Jesus entered our history, our earthly, bodily, gritty history. The critics of Anselm point out how strange an account of salvation is that seems so detached from earthly human existence.

These are weighty criticisms of Anselm's atonement theory. Yet, anyone who reads Anselm with some measure of sympathy comes away with the unmistakable impression that Anselm was a Christian believer of considerable depth, passion, and gratitude. In addition, Anselm's atonement theory captures an important biblical perspective: salvation is accomplished by God's plan and Jesus' faithful obedience, not by human effort or achievement.

The Problem of a Lack of Love
and the Solution of Perfect Love

A younger contemporary of Anselm, the brilliant and compulsive Abelard, is credited with another understanding of how we are saved. Abelard, a popular teacher and clergyman at Notre Dame cathedral in Paris, lived in the home of another cathedral cleric named Fulbert.

Abelard, at the height of his fame, fell in love with the niece of Fulbert, a gifted young woman named Héloïse. They conceived a child and the affair was discovered. Furious, Fulbert attacked Abelard and had him emasculated. Even a calamity of this seriousness, though, did not end the scholarly life of either Abelard or Héloïse. They both retreated from the scandal and took up cloistered life. Abelard became a monk and Héloïse a nun. They wrote many letters to each other that reveal a relationship of shared intellectual interests and spiritual encouragement. It is a remarkable story.

The contribution that Abelard made to atonement theology carries the label "moral influence theory." According to Abelard, the problem with humanity is a lack of love for God and for one another. Jesus came, in his life and his death, and convincingly demonstrated the love of God to undeserving people. This has a powerful effect on people. Their love is awakened, their virtue increases, and they are made whole once again.

Abelard, like Anselm, asks the basic questions of "why" salvation is necessary and "how" salvation works. He says, "A most pressing problem obtrudes itself at this point, as to what that redemption of ours through the death of Christ may be, and in what way the apostle declares that we are justified by his blood."[3] Then Abelard gives an explanation of the saving effect of Christ's death that is quite different from Anselm's. He says, "Now it seems to us that we have been justified by the blood of Christ and reconciled to God in this way: through this unique act of grace manifested to us—in that his Son has taken upon himself our nature and preserved therein in teaching us by word and example even unto death—he has more fully bound us to himself by love; with the result that our hearts should be enkindled by such a gift of divine grace, and true charity should not now shrink from doing anything for him."[4]

Abelard's view of how the death of Christ effects salvation is preserved in some familiar hymns. "When I Survey the Wondrous Cross," by Isaac Watts, is one example:

---

[3] Peter Abelard, "Exposition of the Epistle to the Romans," in Fairweather, *A Scholastic Miscellany*, 280.

[4] Abelard, "Exposition," 283.

> When I survey the wondrous cross
> On which the Prince of glory died,
> My richest gain I count by loss,
> And pour contempt on all my pride.

In this hymn text, the author makes the connection between the death of Jesus Christ and an emotional response in the believer. Jesus' death prompts certain responses, like humility, and other virtues of charity and gratitude.

For Abelard, and other moral-influence theologians, the power of the cross is not in a balance of divine honor. The cross is not saving because an evil army is defeated or a huge ransom payment is made. Abelard found the notion of Christ's death as the necessary cost to restore divine honor outrageous. "How cruel and wicked it seems that anyone should demand the blood of an innocent person as the price for anything, or that it should in any way please him that an innocent man should be slain—still less that God should consider the death of his Son so agreeable that by it he should be reconciled to the whole world!"[5] Abelard, rather, sees the power of Christ's death on the cross in how it changes the human heart. The human heart is moved, warmed, motivated to true love of God.

Stories that illustrate the moral-influence theory tend to be hopelessly sentimental. It strikes us as naive to imagine the cross transforming our hardheartedness to warmheartedness. Even so, there are people who report their genuine conversion in just this sort of language. One story is told by a certain bishop of Paris about a parish priest who encountered some rowdy teenaged boys in the darkened church one evening. They were anything but pious youngsters; they were there only out of boredom. They were goading each other, as adolescents do, in this case to mock the faith they thought was beneath them. The parish priest entered the sanctuary to catch them at their juvenile blasphemies. He collared one of them and said, "Young man, I challenge you. I challenge you to go to the altar and kneel before the crucifix. Look into the eyes of Christ and say, 'You died for me and I don't give a damn.' The young man went, knelt, and looked up at the altar, but the words

---

[5] Ibid.

never came. "I know this to be true," said the bishop, "because I was that young man."

Stories of how the cross changes human hearts tend to be a bit rose-tinted. But many Christians can look back on the development of their faith and recall experiences of being deeply moved by the lengths God was willing to go for us and our salvation.

The Problem of Breaking the Law
and the Solution of Judgment

One of the toughest problems in thinking about salvation is the connection between judgment and grace. One of the assumptions that lies deep at the heart of Christian atonement theology is that *there is a problem,* and that the death and resurrection of Jesus *solves* that problem. God judges the problem, pronouncing a divine no, and God provides the solution, pronouncing a divine yes.

But it is not easy sorting this out. There are complicated and paradoxical connections between judgment and grace. Some of the most deeply familiar, yet deeply difficult, themes cluster around the no and yes of divine judgment and grace. These include lawbreaking, guilty verdict, substitution of punishment, and Jesus' voluntary sacrifice of himself. These images are hurtful and offensive to some Christians sensitive to issues of violence and anything that might appear to sanction it. The same images are comforting to others. Believers who want to think carefully about their faith often feel pulled between two sides in a political struggle.

The background of much of the current debate over atonement images can be seen in the sixteenth century, during the time of the Protestant Reformation. Although the Reformers explicitly attempted to root their theological reflections in Scripture and the earliest centuries of the church, they had their own unique context. For example, the sixteenth century saw the rise of the nation-state. The rule of law became an increasingly crucial component of the emerging nations of Europe.

The way Christian thinkers understood salvation began to be impacted by these prevailing concepts of law. The predicament of human beings was expressed in terms of law. People have broken the law of God. When divine law is broken, punishment must follow. Jesus Christ takes on himself the punishment that people deserve, in his life of obedience to God and especially in his death on the cross. Because the punishment has been carried out on Jesus, the substitute, humanity is freed from the penalty of the law. In briefest scope, this is the atonement theology that has had an enormous influence on Christian theology over the last five hundred years.

This account is not unlike Anselm's version, although Anselm proposes an alternative open to God: either punishment *or* satisfaction. The theory we are now examining assumes only punishment is adequate to deal with breaking God's law. It understands Jesus' death as God's punishment substituted for human sin. This theory is often called the penal substitutionary theory of the atonement.

It may seem to some people that this theory casts God as a cold and heartless judge, demanding punishment for infraction of the divine law. The penal substitutionary theory of the atonement, in fact, arouses strong feelings in people, both in support of this classically understood theory and in angry rejection of it. Some women have seen this classic understanding of the atonement as a tacit legitimation of the abuse of women. There is no doubt that abusers use the Bible, or their perverse understanding of the Bible, to justify battering their wives or partners. They claim that the Bible supports the man as head of the home. They say that the man sometimes has to "punish" the woman, just as God had to "punish" Christ. They command their wives and children to "be like Jesus," obedient and submissive, accepting of pain and suffering. It is, perhaps, no wonder that some feminist theologians have utterly rejected any traditional understandings of salvation through the death and resurrection of Jesus Christ.

Another reaction against traditional understandings of the atonement come from some African American women theologians. The traditional notion that Jesus Christ *took our place* on the cross, to these theologians, is one plank in a vast cultural structure of demeaning attitudes toward African American women. Black women were forced into surrogacy roles in slavery as "substitute" child-caregivers for the master's children and as "substitute" sexual partners for the master. Dolores Williams, an African American theologian, wonders if substitutionary atonement and substitutionary slavery practices are related in complex and negative ways. She explains "that Jesus represents the ultimate surrogate figure; he stands in the place of someone else: sinful humanity. Surrogacy . . . thus takes on an aura of the sacred. It is therefore fitting and proper for black women to ask whether the image of a surrogate-God has salvific power for black women or whether this image supports and reinforces the exploitation that has accompanied their experience with surrogacy."[6]

The angry, passionate criticisms of traditional forms of Christian doctrine are often difficult for comfortable, privileged Christian people to hear. "Surely, the gospel doesn't legitimate abuse—these arguments are nonsense," they might say. But the hurt and anger of people long oppressed, trivialized, or demeaned must be heard. Often it is these voices of pain and frustration that alert churches to their own cozy, comfortable, and utterly wrong ways of understanding the gospel. Certainly, when the gospel has been twisted to prop up abusive power structures, Christians must resolve to reclaim the genuine good news of the gospel and to reject all understandings of the faith that deal death rather than life.

Calvin is often accused of holding a particularly harsh penal substitutionary concept. In his *Institutes of the Christian Religion,* Calvin does occasionally say things that might lead to this conclusion. For example, he says that "God's righteous curse bars our access to him, and God in his capacity as judge is angry toward us."[7] Yet Calvin also takes pains to state clearly that God's love is the foundation and the motivation of the atonement. He said, "It was not after we were reconciled to him through the blood of his Son that he began to love us. Rather, he has loved us before the world was created."[8] A little farther along in the *Institutes,* Calvin remarks that this particular understanding of the atonement is really quite obvious: "I take it to be a commonplace that if Christ made satisfaction for our sins, if he

6 Dolores Williams, *Sisters in the Wilderness* (Maryknoll, N.Y.: Orbis Books, 1993), 162.
7 John Calvin, *Institutes of the Christian Religion,* ed. John T. McNeill, trans Ford Lewis Battles (Philadelphia: Westminster Press, 1960), 2.15.6.
8 Ibid., 2.16.4.

paid the penalty owed by us, . . . then he acquired salvation for us by his righteousness."[9]

Not every Christian today is as confident as Calvin about images of substitution and satisfaction. Christ substituted for our place. Christ satisfied divine justice. For Calvin, this makes good, obvious, biblical sense. For contemporary Christians, this view of atonement sometimes feels contrived, even mechanical. Robert Farrar Capon particularly dislikes the concept of satisfaction that Calvin inherited from Anselm because it coughs up "a tough little ball of fur" that forgiveness and punishment are inseparably linked.[10] Capon, and others, think that the notion that God *had* to exact a penalty in order to forgive is profoundly confusing to the believer. It brings down a thick fog of fear and revulsion, rather than joy and gratitude for God's grace and mercy.

It must be emphasized that, in developing the themes of satisfaction and substitution, Calvin is taking his cue from the passages of Scripture that give voice to these themes. In support of the notion of substitution, Calvin refers us to Hebrews 9:26, "[Christ] has appeared once for all . . . to remove sin by the sacrifice of himself." Again, he cites Paul's analogy in Galatians 3:13, "Christ . . . [became] a curse for us." The classic 2 Corinthians 5:21 was enormously important to Calvin: "For our sake [God] made him to be sin who knew no sin, so that in him we might become the righteousness of God."

These verses, and others like them, lead Calvin to the conclusion that Christ's death substituted for us, that Christ took upon himself the penalty of our sins. Furthermore, that substitution *satisfied* God. Christ's death, then, righted a terrible wrong. It balanced an unbalanced world. It rescued stranded humanity. It saved us.

Clearly, Calvin thinks that Christ's death was a penal substitutionary act—that Christ took on our punishment and released us from its consequences. But, in a remarkable passage in the *Institutes,* Calvin points out that this atonement explanation has enormous effectiveness for increasing our gratitude to God. Calvin thinks this

---

[9] Ibid., 2.17.3.

[10] Robert Farrar Capon, *The Fingerprints of God: Tracking the Divine Suspect through a History of Images* (Grand Rapids: Wm. B. Eerdmans Publishing Co., 2000), 117.

view is pastorally helpful to people. He would be puzzled by people who reject this particular atonement account as portraying a harsh and judgmental God. Quite the opposite, Calvin thinks.

He imagines the reaction of a person hearing a sort of "general" explanation about salvation through Jesus Christ. In this imaginary scene, a person is told that human sin is a rebellion against God, that people are all terribly estranged from God, but that God has put it all right, bringing us once again into relationship with God. Calvin remarks, "This man . . . will surely experience and feel something of what he owes to God's mercy."[11]

But, continues Calvin in his imagination, think how that person's gratitude would be increased if he or she knew everything!

On the other hand, suppose he learns, as Scripture teaches,
that he was estranged from God through sin,
is an heir of wrath,
subject to the curse of eternal death,
excluded from all hope of salvation,
beyond every blessing of God,
the slave of Satan,
captive under the yoke of sin,
destined finally for a dreadful destruction and already involved in it;
and that at this point Christ interceded as his advocate,
took upon himself and suffered the punishment that, from God's righteous judgement, threatened all sinners;
that he purged with his blood those evils which had rendered sinners hateful to God;
that by this expiation he made satisfaction and sacrifice duly to God the Father;
that as intercessor he has appeased God's wrath;
that on this foundation rests the peace of God with men;
that by this bond his benevolence is maintained toward them.
Will the man not then be even more moved by all these things which so vividly portray the greatness of the calamity from which he has been rescued?[12]

[11] Calvin, *Institutes,* 2.16.2.
[12] Ibid. (italics mine)

Calvin says, in effect, "Knowing all *that,* wouldn't anyone be overwhelmed with gratitude?" This passage reveals an important insight into the way Calvin thought about the faith and how to find the right words to express the faith. Calvin cared about what *effect* his words, his explanations, had on Christian believers. If there was an explanation of salvation that would raise the awe, wonder, and joy of believers, then those are the words which should be used. If other words do not have this effect, then those are not the best words to explain salvation. Calvin cared about the impact or effect of his words on his readers or listeners. His fundamental conviction was that the gift of salvation is such a great gift that people must be able to "get it," to really sense what God's gracious mercy was accomplishing in the cross of Jesus Christ.

Calvin was convinced that a heightened gratitude to God for salvation was achieved with an atonement account that included images of substituted punishment and the appeasement of divine wrath. He says, just a few pages farther on in his atonement section that "trembling consciences find repose only in sacrifice and cleansing by which sins are expiated."[13]

A question immediately arises at this point. What do we do as Christian believers if twenty-first-century consciences are *not* comforted by these images of substituted punishment and sacrifice? Ought we to insist on such images, rooted as they are in Scripture and the Christian tradition, or ought we to find other biblically rooted images that do comfort contemporary people and arouse their hearts to gratitude for God's boundless mercy? This question faces not only theologians, but all Christian believers who want to find the right words to express their faith. They want to find words that really get at the good news of the gospel.

Many Christians, if someone asked them how we are saved through the death of Christ, might stammer out an explanation that bears a resemblance to Calvin's. They might say, "We are saved because Jesus died for us. . . . You know, Jesus took the punishment that we deserved. That's how salvation happens." There is no question that this particular understanding of the cross has been enor-

---

[13] Ibid., 2.16.5.

mously influential, not only in North America, but in many Christian communities around the world. Many Christians simply assume that this version of the cross, which sounds so familiar to them, is the best—perhaps even the only—understanding of the cross. Some well-loved hymns and Scripture texts, such as this ancient hymn attributed to Bernard of Clairvaux, express this understanding.

> O Sacred head, now wounded,
>   With grief and shame weighed down;
> Now scornfully surrounded
>   With thorns, Thine only crown;
> O sacred head, what glory,
>   What bliss till now was Thine!
> Yet, though despised and gory,
>   I joy to call Thee mine.
>
> What Thou, my Lord, hast suffered
>   Was all for sinners' gain:
> Mine, mine was the transgression,
>   But Thine the deadly pain.
> Lo, here I fall, my Savior!
>   'Tis I deserve Thy place;
> Look on me with Thy favor,
>   Vouchsafe to me Thy grace.[14]

The Suffering Servant passages of Isaiah are also important for this image. Isaiah 53:4–6 is a classic text, enormously influential for hymn writers, sacred music composers, theologians, preachers, and countless Christian believers:

> Surely he has borne our infirmities
>   and carried our diseases;
> yet we accounted him stricken,
>   struck down by God, and afflicted.
> But he was wounded for our transgressions,
>   crushed for our iniquities;
> upon him was the punishment that made us whole,
>   and by his bruises we are healed.

---

[14] Trans. James Waddell Alexander, in *The Presbyterian Hymnal* (Louisville, Ky.: Westminster/John Knox Press, 1990), no. 98.

> All we like sheep have gone astray;
>   we have all turned to our own way,
> and the LORD has laid on him
>   the iniquity of us all.

This is a powerful text, one that speaks directly to the terrible dilemma of humanity, burdened by transgression too heavy for us to carry off ourselves. Only the Suffering Servant, read by Christian eyes as a direct reference to Jesus, could bear this punishment. The tragedy and drama of this text has deeply connected with the imaginations and piety of many Christians.

Wendell Berry's short story "Pray without Ceasing" discloses some of these same elements of judgment, suffering, grace, and love. Thad Coulter had killed his best friend in broad daylight on the main street of town because the friend refused to lend him a large sum of money. Thad is arrested and jailed.

Overcome by shame and horror, Thad sits in his jail cell and longs for his own death. But then he receives a single visitor—his daughter, Martha Elizabeth, who walked long miles to see him. When Thad looks up and sees her, he covers his face with his hands. It is not his guilt and shame that make him cover his face. There is that, too, in his soul, so thick and deep it chokes him. But what makes Thad cover his face is something else.

"In that moment, he saw his guilt included in love that stood as near him as Martha Elizabeth and at that moment wore her flesh. . . . Surely God's love includes people who can't bear it."

The narrator of the story says, "People sometimes talk of God's love as if it's a pleasant thing. But it is terrible, in a way. Think of all it includes. It includes Thad Coulter, mean and drunk and foolish, before he killed Mr. Feltner, and it included him afterwards."[15]

Martha Elizabeth is the symbol of Christ in this story. She both judges the sin of her father and yet includes him in her love. When her father saw Martha Elizabeth's love, he felt the truth of what Wendell Berry calls a "terrible love," a love that rejects the sin and yet forgives and accepts the sinner. The Christian faith confesses that it is by this "terrible love" of God that we are forgiven and accepted.

---

[15] Wendel Berry, *Fidelity* (New York: Pantheon Books, 1992), 50.

Self-Improvement or Suffering Solidarity: How Are We Saved? (Part 3)

The seventeenth and eighteenth centuries in Europe and England ushered in seismic cultural changes. Enormous advances were made in the natural sciences. Galileo (1564–1642) demonstrated the truth of Copernicus's theory of a sun-centered planetary system, and people no longer could think of themselves as literally the center of the universe. Newton (1642–1727), who was born the year Galileo died, proposed that the world operated according to set and predictable laws, including gravity and motion. By the beginning of the eighteenth century, astronomers, biologists, mathematicians, and natural philosophers had utterly transformed human beings' understandings of their world. It was confidently assumed that the human mind had unlocked the secrets of the world. The world's laws were stated, measured, and proved. Human confidence in the powers of reason and science were at an all time high.

The Problem of Irrationality and the Rational Jesus

During this time of momentous scientific advances, religion seemed to be spiraling downhill. Religious wars and persecutions caused untold suffering. The Thirty Years' War, a complex political and religious struggle from 1618 to 1648, engulfed Europe and destroyed as much as 20 percent of the population, especially in Germany. Exhausted by the brutality of war and the seemingly petty religious issues that sparked armed conflict, thinkers began to ask whether Christianity made any sense. Was it reasonable? Was it rational?

Some seventeenth- and eighteenth-century thinkers believed they could present the Christian religion in concepts that were utterly reasonable. Faith would be measured according to the standard of reason. Only concepts and principles that could pass that standard would be considered appropriate for assent, for belief. Using this method, Lord Herbert of Cherbury, a seventeenth-century British gentleman, believed he had discovered the true essence of the faith. There are five rational principles that can guide all people to the truth, without bloody conflict and schism. The principles seemed obvious to Lord Herbert and his followers, who became known as deists. "God exists" is one principle that seemed to his Lordship obvious to all rational people. Another is, "God ought to be worshiped." Another states that people have an obligation to repent of their sins, to shape up. That's only rational, obvious, sensible.

Nowhere in Lord Herbert's list is there any mention of Jesus Christ and his saving life, death, and resurrection. This part of the Christian story was not obviously rational to him. Neither, strictly speaking, was this part of the Christian story really necessary. People are responsible for their own wrongs. They did them. They have to fix them. This is rational religion at its simplest.

Of course, not everyone in the seventeenth and eighteenth centuries was a deist. Without question, there were uncounted scores of Christian believers, Protestants and Catholics, who continued to believe, as Christians had for centuries, in a God far greater and more mysterious than human rationality could possibly grasp. But many Christian thinkers, influenced by the Enlightenment and its stress on human reason, had a view of human flourishing that rested more on human self-reliance than on God's grace.

An Enlightenment view of Jesus Christ, then, did not use the language of salvation or atonement. Rather, it considered Jesus as the best example of a truly rational person. Jesus had a rich and full consciousness of God, a consciousness that gave him the ability to live a virtuous and self-aware life. The great nineteenth-century theologian Friedrich Schleiermacher showed some Enlightenment influences when he said, "The Redeemer assumes the believers into the fellowship of His unclouded blessedness, and this is His reconciling activity."[1]

Another rational-religion emphasis was on the love of Jesus. Clearly, Jesus cared deeply about other people. Righteousness was his operating principle. Hypocrisy and injustice were denounced. If people could just be more like Jesus, if they could live a truly rational, virtuous life, then they would live up to their human potential. Salvation is not really the issue. Rather, the issues are education, knowledge, virtue, and maximizing human potential. These are what people need.

Such an optimistic view of people and people's ability to take their problems in hand seemed, for a while, to fit the astonishing advances in science and technology from the seventeenth century to the early twentieth century. The long list of scientific break-throughs made the powers of the human intellect seem invincible: Refrigeration. Electricity. Telegraph and telephone. Steam engines. The cotton gin. Music and art displayed human achievement in spectacular variety and richness as well: Bach, Haydn, Mozart, Beethoven, van Gogh, Monet, Coleridge, Wordsworth, Goethe. Human achievement made salvation seem downright unnecessary.

But these examples of human achievement are only part of the story. The same centuries that saw such spectacular growth of human knowledge also saw the institutionalization of slavery in America and the rise of child labor in damp factories and dark mines in Britain. The same century that displayed such sharp criticism of religion also gave birth to waves of revival in America and England. To assume that the Enlightenment was the only intellectual and cultural impulse of the seventeenth and eighteenth centuries would be to ignore strong, deep streams in the broad Christian river. The Puritans, the Pietists, the Wesleyans, the African American slaves, and many others are important exceptions to the impulses of the Enlightenment. Clearly, this is a complex period of time.

---

[1] Friedrich Schleiermacher, *The Christian Faith* (Edinburgh: T. & T. Clark, 1989), 431.

The Enlightenment's emphasis on human potential and self-sufficiency still influences us today. But the naive optimism of the Enlightenment was shattered in the two world wars of the twentieth century. The trenches and gas masks of World War I and the concentration camps and atomic bombs of World War II destroyed forever the illusion that human beings could move upward and onward toward an idyllic future.

Confessing the Faith Today

Many of the images and explanations of salvation that have been described in this and the two preceding chapters are still around today. They are in our hymns, sermons, prayers, and liturgies. We hear of Jesus as a mighty conqueror, destroying the power of evil. We hear of Jesus as the perfect satisfaction for the weight of our sins. We hear of Jesus as bearing the punishment that our breaking of God's law requires. We hear of Jesus as the premier example of human dignity and wisdom.

But the enormous shocks of the twentieth century have brought to the surface some new understandings of Jesus' death and resurrection for Christian believers. Although all the old images still operate in Christian thinking, devotion, hymns, and prayers, there are several recent images of Jesus Christ that seek to address the predicament of humanity in fresh, contemporary ways. One of those images is of Jesus as the liberator of people long oppressed and demeaned by unjust political and economic systems. Jesus is on the side of the poor and homeless. Jesus takes up the cause of the orphan and the unemployed. Jesus is on the side of the single mother in Chicago, the undocumented worker in California's Central Valley, the young girl sold into the sex industry in Indonesia. Jesus cares about people with AIDS in San Francisco and South Africa.

Because Jesus suffered injustice in his life too, a unique connection exists between all suffering people and Jesus. In Jesus' sufferings and death, all sufferings and deaths are included. Sufferers sometimes find some measure of comfort and solidarity in reflecting on Christ's sufferings. Jesus knows. He understands.

But sufferers mainly want to stop suffering. They yearn for someone to come and rescue them, to right the wrong, to hold back destructive and cruel powers that engulf them. How do the cross and resurrection of Jesus help now, in this injustice, in the midst of this suffering? Suffering people look to Jesus as the source of their liberation, especially through the resurrection. The cross is the symbol of all the hatred, violence, and sin of the world. There it is concentrated. The empty tomb is God's sign of hope, hope that in God's future all tears will be wiped away and peace and wholeness will once again grace God's good earth. Jesus once said to his disciples, "You will suffer in the world. But take courage. I have overcome the world" (John 16:33 alt.). Even though the world is filled with pain, grief, and injustice, God in Christ *will* ultimately triumph over the evil that seems so often to gain the advantage.

The Problem of Oppression and the Solution of Liberation

A vigorous expression of atonement images of freedom and justice is seen in the diverse and widespread liberation theology movement in the last third of the twentieth century. Located primarily in Central and South America, liberation theology took its inspiration from the prophetic literature of the Old Testament, where the prophets denounce political and economic injustice and call for God's people to join in God's care for the poor. They also looked to the Gospels, where Jesus is clearly portrayed as the friend of sinners and outcasts. The poor, the prostitutes, the tax collectors, the mentally ill, the homeless—these were Jesus' kind of people.

Liberation theology rooted and flourished in communities of poor people. When these people heard the biblical prophets denounce unjust land distribution, corrupt courts, and exorbitant interest rates for the poor, they knew that God cares about their situations of oppression too. When they heard from their local priest or minister the Gospel stories of Jesus, it was as if Jesus was walking in their own village, caring for their sick, their poor. Archbishop Oscar Romero's murder, as he was celebrating mass, on March 24, 1980, became a powerful symbol for liberation theology. If Bishop

Romero's enemies hoped that his murder would extinguish the good news of God's care for the poor, they vastly underestimated the power of the gospel.

Liberation theology is convinced that the Christian faith requires suffering for the sake of justice. One liberation theologian, Leonardo Boff, a Franciscan priest who was born and now teaches theology in Brazil, once said, "To preach the cross today is to preach the following of Jesus. . . . And to follow Jesus is to take his path, pursue his cause, and achieve his victory."[2] God does not wish us to sit around and wait for the coming of the kingdom of God. God calls us to join in the cause of the kingdom, to feed the hungry, advocate for the orphan and the widow, and live in the victory of the resurrection. Liberation theology looks expectantly to the future, when God will break into history and restore harmony and justice. In the meantime, there's work to be done, in Jesus' name.

Liberation theologians think that the Christian tradition has often been concerned more with being "saved from sin" than with being saved from oppression and injustice. It has been far too easy, they say, for powerful, comfortable people to push aside questions about social structures of injustice and talk instead about sin. Liberation theology has issued a powerful and prophetic reminder that sin and injustice are blood brothers.

Sin and injustice are not synonyms, however. Sin includes more than injustice. It includes what might be called "everyday sins," like lying, envying, lusting, and cheating. It includes such "minor sins" as speeding, complaining, and bullying, although the ripples that spread out from such sins often pollute more distant shores than we know. It includes headliner sins like murder, betrayal, and all violence. It also includes what is sometimes called "systemic sin"—the rotten core of many political structures and economic systems.

Certainly, political and economic injustice falls in the broad category of sins that Jesus liberates us from. To suggest that the death

---

[2] Leonardo Boff, *Passion of Christ: Passion of the World* (Maryknoll, N.Y.: Orbis Books, 1989), 132.

and resurrection of Jesus save us from sins of selfishness and swearing, but not from sins of ecological destruction or cultural indifference to the millions of people dying of AIDS in Africa, is clearly to limit the claims of the Christian faith. An important liberation theology document from the Medellín, Colombia, conference of Catholic bishops in 1968 gives a statement of Jesus as liberator. The document says, "It is the same God who, in the fullness of time, sends his Son in the flesh, so that he might come to liberate all people from all slavery to which sin has subjected them: hunger, misery, oppression, and ignorance."[3]

Liberation theology understands the cross of Jesus as a divine monument to all the victims of oppression, genocide, displacement, war, and famine. The cross announces that, for God, all suffering counts. The suffering of Jesus and the suffering of human persons throughout the centuries matter to God. Yet suffering can only be overcome, paradoxically, through the cross and resurrection. The cross is where Jesus took on the burden of humanity's violence and injustice. A symbol of violence, the cross yet announces the end of violence. The empty tomb announces that the same God who raised Jesus from the dead will someday conquer death itself and put an end to all suffering.

The Problem of Alienation and the Solution of Healing

Another recent salvation image that expresses the longings of modern people is the image of healing. What is wrong with frantic, stressed modern people? They are alienated, filled with despair and anxiety. They worry about their children's safety in a media-soaked culture that glorifies violence. They worry about their job security in an economy that discards workers for the sake of the profit margin. They worry about their pension, medical insurance, and escalating college tuitions. Sociologist David Myers reports in his book *The American Paradox* that people have more money, but less happiness. They have their expensive cars, summer homes,

[3] Quoted in Gustavo Gutiérrez, *A Theology of Liberation* (Maryknoll, N.Y.: Orbis Books, 1973), 103.

and electronic gadgets, but they long for satisfaction, joy, and hope. Myers says, "We now have, as average Americans, doubled real incomes and doubled what money buys. We have espresso coffee, the World Wide Web, sport utility vehicles, and caller ID. And we have less happiness, more depression, more fragile relationships, less communal commitment, less vocational security, more crime (even after the recent decline) and more demoralized children."[4]

If this is the predicament of the affluent, the educated, the upwardly mobile, then salvation is understood in the terms of Luke's Gospel, Jesus as the great healer. Jesus is the healer of all the wounds of our human condition. Jesus heals our loneliness, our alienation, our despair. In a world that is so bereft of community, Jesus offers friendship. In a world brimming with despair, Jesus offers hope. In a world weighted with depression, Jesus offers comfort.

As helpful as this perspective is for many contemporary Christians, it must not be reduced to a cozy and sentimental faith. A bumper sticker declares, "You are too blessed to be depressed." Here, the Christian faith is portrayed as a quick antidote to a serious and complex medical condition. It may well be that, by the grace of God, faith can be a lifeline for a depressed person. But the Christian faith is neither a prescription nor a placebo. Believers can and do suffer from depression, cancer, and unemployment. In some places in the world, believers suffer severe persecution for their faith. The gospel does not protect us from suffering. It does, however, give us the confidence that God will, in God's good time, restore all creation to full peace and harmony.

Finding the Right Words

"Jesus died for our sins." This simple statement expresses the core of the message of the New Testament. A handful of atonement options surveyed in this book have tried to explain some of the

---

[4] David G. Myers, *The American Paradox: Spiritual Hunger in an Age of Plenty* (New Haven, Conn.: Yale University Press, 2000), xi.

ways that Christians have understood this statement for nearly two thousand years. The very fact that there are a variety of atonement options presents some persistent problems, however.

For one thing, none of the options are completely satisfactory by themselves. No doubt early Christians who understood salvation to result from a cosmic battle between God and evil wondered, But how does this really work? Perhaps medieval Christians who assumed that human sin had offended God's honor and must be dealt with through punishment or satisfaction still puzzled over how Jesus' death really accomplishes this. We can imagine that a rational Enlightenment thinker was not completely confident in the powers of human reason every day. Perhaps in the middle of long, sleepless nights, he yearned for more, for a God who so loved the world that God sent the well-loved Son into the world to save the world from sin and self-destruction. Perhaps some contemporary Christians, too, so steeped in a thinned out "Jesus and me" spirituality, suspect there must be more to the significance of Jesus than the boundaries of their own experience. There is no single explanation that can adequately express the core Christian conviction in Jesus Christ as Lord.

Yet, another problem immediately arises. The simple fact that there are so many atonement explanations might suggest that there is no actual content to the Christian confession in Jesus Christ. Some people think *this*. Other people think *that*. It is hard to know how to reconcile dramatically different understandings of the cross. When the long Christian tradition sees the cross of Christ at one time as a cosmic battle between God and evil and, at another time, as a healing for the alienations of humanity, then the problem of the content of the faith must at least be faced.

A third problem with a list of atonement explanations comes from the very notion of an "explanation" for the cross of Christ. A perceptive theologian once said that atonement theories are like putting "roses on the cross." They make the scandal and horror of the cross look pretty, charming, decorative. Nice theological theories of the atonement manage to avoid the way things really are. The fact is, we cannot reconcile ourselves to God. Only God can bring a sinful and broken humanity back to God. This is how it is. And God has accomplished this reconciliation, possible only by God's own love and grace, through the life, death, and resurrection of Jesus Christ.

Writer Anne Lamott once remarked that she has only two prayers: "Help, help, help" and "Thank you, thank you, thank you." This reminds us of the starting point of all theology. We cannot attempt to explain the precise logic or mechanics of salvation. We respond to salvation out of our need for God's grace and our gratitude for that grace. Christians have long realized that the truth of the cross and resurrection of Jesus Christ is far bigger than their grammars and vocabularies are capable of holding. It is a truth that bursts the limited boundaries of our imaginations and our understanding. It is a truth that even bursts the limited boundaries of our hopes and dreams. Our theories and notions and doctrines about Jesus are painfully inadequate. Theological language creaks and groans under the strain of the enormity of the truth it attempts to express.

Perhaps only the writer of the book of Revelation, at the very end of the New Testament, dreamed big enough about Jesus Christ. His visions of the slain and risen Christ are filled with strange, wild imagery. In Revelation 4–5, a heavenly scene is described that is more elaborate and grand than a magnificent opera stage. There are an emerald rainbow, gold crowns, flashes of lightning, rumbles of thunder, blazing lamps, a great throne, and a sea of glass. Occupying this scene are four living creatures, twenty-four elders, and uncounted hosts of angels. All sing in chorus to the Lamb, the crucified and risen Jesus Christ. "Worthy is the Lamb!" they all sing, "power and wealth and wisdom and might and honor and glory and blessing." All are received by the Lamb, who was slain and now lives in the heavenly realms, worshiped and glorified by all creation. In other scenes in Revelation, there are earthquakes, a beast, a dragon, and a holy city with all the nations of the earth streaming into it. Far from being a coded document with hidden details about the end of the world, the book of Revelation is a bold and dramatic hymn of praise to Jesus Christ. All the incredible characters of the book of Revelation at least remind us that our words, our concepts, our doctrines are not adequate to the task of expressing the love of God in Jesus Christ our Lord.

But even a keen awareness of the limits of language does not stop believers from trying to find the right words to speak their faith. When the apostles Peter and John in the early days of the Christian community were instructed sternly by local officials not to talk about Jesus, they answered, "We cannot keep from speaking about what we have seen and heard" (Acts 4:20). Christians today, as well, must speak about what they have seen and heard. They do this in a variety of ways. Prayer, worship, teaching their children the great truths of the faith, reaching out in service, witness, and love to those who do not know Jesus—all these are ways of giving voice to the faith.

One of the documents of the Presbyterian Church (U.S.A.), the Confession of 1967, says this about Jesus our Savior:

> God's reconciling act in Jesus Christ is a mystery which the Scriptures describe in various ways. It is called the sacrifice of a lamb, a shepherd's life given for his sheep, atonement by a priest; again it is ransom of a slave, payment of debt, vicarious satisfaction of a legal penalty, and victory over the powers of evil. These are expressions of a truth which remains beyond the reach of all theory in the depths of God's love for [humanity]. They reveal the gravity, cost, and sure achievement of God's reconciling work.[5]

It is no accident that the Christian tradition contains a range and variety of atonement explanations. A single explanation cannot bear the weight of accounting for the truth of God's love for a lost world. Yet, it is also no accident that all atonement theories attempt to express the heart of the gospel. Each atonement account has its own "read" on the truth of the gospel. Each has its strengths, as well as clear weaknesses.

The cosmic-battle image makes clear that the principalities and powers of darkness are formidable opponents to the love of

---

[5] See *The Constitution of the Presbyterian Church (U.S.A.),* Part I, *Book of Confessions* (Louisville, Ky.: Office of the General Assembly, Presbyterian Church (U.S.A.), 1999), 9.09.

God. Yet, God's love does prevail in Jesus Christ. The ransom image emphasizes that sin traps us in prisons of our own making. The satisfaction image, expressed by Anselm in the medieval age, reminds us that Jesus' death was an event of divine self-giving. It is only through God's ingenious and effective plan that a desperately indebted humanity can be free. The judicial language of Calvin, with punishments and verdicts dominating the imagery, language that provokes such negative responses in some Christians today, does not allow us to forget that human sin is a terrible violation of the will of God for human persons. Calvin was convinced that this strong language of punishment and substitution is the only thing that can truly evoke in us the kind of gratitude appropriate for such a great act of God.

Each atonement image that has served the church in the past two thousand years has a particular "slant" on the gospel. But the very heart of the gospel is perhaps no better expressed than in five compact verses, 2 Corinthians 5:17–21:

> So if anyone is in Christ, there is a new creation: everything old has passed away; see, everything has become new! All this is from God, who reconciled us to himself through Christ, and has given us the ministry of reconciliation; that is, in Christ God was reconciling the world to himself, not counting their trespasses against them, and entrusting the message of reconciliation to us. So we are ambassadors for Christ, since God is making his appeal through us; we entreat you on behalf of Christ, be reconciled to God. For our sake he made him to be sin who knew no sin, so that in him we might become the righteousness of God.

This great summary of the faith contains three important affirmations. First, through Jesus Christ, all things are made new. The old order of sin and death and suffering has been overcome. A new reality now exists.

The new reality that has replaced the old is illustrated in a short story by Flannery O'Connor. Somewhat awkwardly entitled "The Artificial Nigger," the story uses a hated and demeaning symbol of racism to portray the inbreaking of a new reality.

The story is told of a little boy named Nelson and his grandfather, Mr. Head. The grandfather is an angry and bitter man, who belittles Nelson. The boy hates and despises him. Nelson and Mr. Head live in rural Georgia, but have taken a train to Atlanta early one morning. When they get to Atlanta, they soon get lost. Twice, black people try to help, but Mr. Head cannot recognize the mercy that is extended to him by these strangers, and in despair, the two collapse on a curb on some nameless Atlanta street. When they finally ask for help and are on their way to the train station to go home, they see a "lawn jockey," what they called "an artificial nigger." It, too, is broken down a bit and is tilting awkwardly, a figure that looks more like the crucified Christ than a carefree symbol of a misremembered past. It is there, at the foot of this cross, that Nelson and Mr. Head become a new creation.

The story continues:

> The two of them stood there with their necks forward at almost the same angle and their shoulders curved in almost exactly the same way. . . . Mr. Head looked like an ancient child and Nelson like a miniature old man. They stood gazing at the artificial Negro as if they were faced with some great mystery, some monument to another's victory that brought them together in their common defeat. They could both feel it dissolving their differences like an action of mercy. Mr. Head had never known before what mercy felt like because he had been too good to deserve any. . . . He understood [that mercy] was all a man could carry into death to give his Maker and he suddenly burned with shame that he had so little of it to take with him. He stood appalled, judging himself with the thoroughness of God, while the action of mercy covered his pride like a flame and consumed it. . . . He realized that he was forgiven for sins from the beginning of time . . . until the present, when he had denied poor Nelson. He saw that no sin was too monstrous for him to claim as his own, and since God loved in proportion as [God] forgave, he felt ready at that instant to enter Paradise.[6]

---

[6] Flannery O'Connor, "The Artificial Nigger," in *The Complete Stories* (New York: Noonday Press, 1972), 268–70.

An object of racial domination, a lawn statue of a black jockey, is an image of the cross of Christ in O'Connor's story. For Mr. Head, the broken and tilted lawn statue both revealed his own sin and brokenness and then overcame it. At one and the same time, he was exposed for who he truly was and transformed into a new creation. The scandal of using a visible racial slur to stand for the cross of Christ is O'Connor's shocking way of highlighting the radical love of God.

The second affirmation from the 2 Corinthians 5 text is that God sent Jesus Christ for this purpose. "All this is from God," says verse 18. The life and teachings and death and resurrection of Jesus Christ—all this is *for us* and *from God*. Jesus is no accidental Savior. He was sent by God to be the Savior. He willingly took up the task of bringing reconciliation to a world crushed by sin. Martin Luther King Jr., in his Nobel Prize acceptance speech, said, "Calvary is a telescope through which we look into the long vista of eternity and see the love of God breaking into time. Out of the hugeness of his generosity, God allowed his only-begotten Son to die that we may live."[7] Not only did God allow the only-begotten Son to die that we may live, but Jesus himself chose to undertake the enormous burden of taking on the sins of the world so that the world might take on the righteousness of God.

The image of "trading places" in 2 Corinthians 5:21, "For our sake he made him to be sin who knew no sin, so that in him we might become the righteousness of God," is sometimes called the "wonderful exchange." It is spelled out more completely by a sixteenth-century preacher strongly convinced of the love of God. John Calvin describes a whole series of "exchanges" that Christ makes with us. Each of these liberate us and free us for new life. He said that God, in Christ, became the "Son of man" so that we could be sons and daughters of God. Jesus descended to earth so that we might ascend to heaven. Jesus took on mortality so that we might take on immortality. Jesus took on our weaknesses so that we might be strengthened. Jesus took on our poverty so that we

---

[7] Martin Luther King Jr., *A Testament of Hope: The Essential Writings and Speeches of Martin Luther King Jr.,* ed. James Washington (New York: Harper & Row, 1986), 224.

might receive all the riches of God. Finally, Jesus took on our sins so that we might receive God's righteousness.[8]

The "wonderful exchange" idea is helpful in thinking about the cross. It makes clear that we cannot save ourselves. It makes clear that Jesus had to take up our deepest failures, sins, and brokenness in order to overcome them and transform us into new creatures. It makes clear that all this happened *from God* and *for us*.

The third point of the 2 Corinthians 5 text is that God entrusts us with the task of being the ambassadors of reconciliation to the whole world. We have been reconciled. It is not something we can keep to ourselves. We are called to be the messengers of God's reconciliation so that all may hear.

These three themes from the compact text in 2 Corinthians do not solve all the questions surrounding the cross. Big issues remain. Why was a death necessary for this reconciliation to happen? Could God have done this another way? Here it is important to remember that the challenge for believers is not to prove to a skeptical audience the solid logic of the cross. As a matter of fact, the cross does not make sense. It is strange and peculiar that we are brought into fellowship with God through the odd combination of a botched trial, a hasty execution, and a miraculous resurrection. The cross and empty tomb do not save because of our convincing explanations. The cross and empty tomb save because God has chosen them to be the means of our reconciliation to God and to one another.

It is not an evasion, then, for a Christian to say, "Well, I'm not exactly sure how salvation works. But I am convinced it does." And then, she might make an attempt at an explanation. "You see, it is something like a wonderful exchange. It is something like a mighty victory. It is something like liberation." The long history of atonement explanations comes from believers trying to find the right words.

---

[8] Calvin, *Institutes,* ed. John T. McNeill, trans. Ford Lewis Battles (Philadelphia: Westminster Press, 1960), 4.17.2.

Brokenheartedness and Hope: What Difference Does It Make?

*E*verything that has been said so far is worthless unless it makes a real difference in the lives of people. It is no good to talk about "everything [becoming] new" in Jesus Christ if ethnic groups are still torn apart by hatred, lives are destroyed by betrayal, societies are weakened by injustice. The community that confesses faith in Jesus Christ must reflect the actual reality of salvation.

The story is told of a child who once asked a professor if he was saved. The professor, perhaps typically, asked for a clarification. "Do you mean to ask me if I *was* saved or if I *am being* saved or if I *will be* saved?" The question is a good one. Past, present, and future—all are included in the time line of salvation. In one sense, Jesus Christ saved us once for all on the cross and through the empty tomb. In this sense, the past tense, salvation means that God took up all the despair and sin that destroys human beings into God's own divine life and overcame it. Not content to be a God far away from us, God willed to become one with us, taking on even the worst of human hatred and injustice, in order to restore us. This happened in the past, decisively, through Jesus Christ's death and resurrection.

In another sense, Jesus Christ saves us now, for new life, in thanks and praise to God. Simply put, salvation in the present tense means that believers follow Jesus. People should be able to notice the difference it makes to be a Christian. The community of believers, who gather together for worship and service, must visibly embody the gospel. In the ways we live and speak and act, Christ himself is present among us, through the power of the Holy Spirit.

The apostle John, in the New Testament, never tired of reminding the early Christians that unbelievers notice how Christians act. They draw conclusions about the truth of the gospel based on the behavior of the community. When people look at Christians, at the ways they worship God and serve one another, they will say to each other, "Look! See how they love one another!" (see 1 John 3). Or, people will see the hatred among Christians, their divisiveness, their indifference to the poor, and their smugness, and they will conclude that the faith is nothing more than a crutch for self-satisfaction and a prop for pride. John remarks, "Those who say, 'I love God,' and hate their brothers or sisters, are liars; for those who do not love a brother or sister whom they have seen, cannot love God whom they have not seen" (1 John 4:20).

One of the most dramatic stories of visibly living the gospel in the present is told by Philip Hallie, in his book *Lest Innocent Blood Be Shed: The Story of the Village of Le Chambon and How Goodness Happened There.* Hallie tells the story of a French Reformed pastor in Southern France during the perilous years of Nazi occupation. The pastor, André Trocmé, and his congregation organized together to save the lives of thousands of Jews by hiding them in secret shelters and hidden rooms in their own homes. These "righteous Gentiles," as Jewish Holocaust survivors call Christians like these, show concretely what difference it makes to be saved. Theologian George Hunsinger suggests three specific virtues that Trocmé and his congregation practiced in those dangerous years.[1]

First, they practiced *an ethic of watchfulness.* Alert to both the blatant and the subtle patterns of evil and oppression, the people of the Le Chambon congregation watched carefully for the perverse propaganda of the anti-Semitic press and refused to be poisoned by it. Hallie reports that Pastor Trocmé "believed that 'decent' people who stay inactive out of cowardice or indifference

---

[1] George Hunsinger, *Disruptive Grace* (Grand Rapids: Wm. B. Eerdmans Publishing Co., 2000), 109–13. I am indebted to Hunsinger's perceptive analysis of the Le Chambon story.

when around them human beings are being humiliated and destroyed are the most dangerous people in the world."[2]

Second, the small congregation practiced *an ethic of noncompliance*. In other words, they were not cooperative! When Trocmé was instructed by a church official to stop sheltering Jews, Trocmé refused, knowing his allegiance was not primarily to church authorities, but to Jesus. Hallie reports a specific conversation remembered by Trocmé:

Church official: What I want to say is this: you must stop helping refugees.

      Trocmé: Do you realize what you are asking? These people, especially the Jews, are in very great danger. If we do not shelter them or take them across the mountains to Switzerland, they may well die.

Church official: What you are doing is endangering the very existence not only of this village but of the Protestant church of France! You must stop helping them.

      Trocmé: If we stop, many of them will starve to death, or die of exposure, or be deported and killed. We cannot stop.

Church official: You must stop. The marshal will take care of them. He will see to it that they are not hurt.

      Trocmé: No.[3]

Third, the congregation practiced *an ethic of fidelity and witness*. In other words, they were faithful to Jesus Christ and, by their actions, witnessed to the cross of Christ. Faithfulness to Jesus Christ meant a willingness to go against all conventional wisdom, all cultural assumptions, all human authority. Trocmé was convinced that he and his church had to follow Jesus in the same path of nonviolence and forgiveness that Jesus himself walked.

---

[2] Philip P. Hallie, *Lest Innocent Blood Be Shed: The Story of the Village of Le Chambon and How Goodness Happened There* (New York: Harper & Row, 1979), 266.

[3] Hallie, *Lest Innocent Blood,* 143.

The Le Chambon congregation demonstrated that salvation is not only a past event. Salvation is lived out in the real circumstances and challenges of life. Being "saved" means we pattern our lives after Jesus. The church is the gathered community, the place where the truth of the gospel is actually lived out. Jesus Christ is present with his church, through the Spirit, in the preaching of the Word and in the sacraments. Far more than being a dispenser of religious goods and services, the church actually embodies all that the gospel proclaims. The church both proclaims and lives an alternate vision of reality. Here is the place where justice and peace are practiced, where virtues are lived out, where love binds together people who have been long separated.

A New Testament scholar describes how the apostle Paul imagined this community: "Paul's church is not an aggregate of justified sinners or a sacramental institute or a means for private self-sanctification but the avant-garde of the new creation in a hostile world, creating beachheads in this world of God's dawning new world and yearning for the day of God's visible lordship over his creation, the general resurrection of the dead."[4] The location of such beachheads in this world that anticipate the dawn of God's new world are Christian congregations in their own unique, particular place. A downtown Atlanta congregation may be a beachhead of justice for the poor and homeless. A rural Iowa congregation may be a beachhead of identity and hope for farmers who are losing their farms to mega-techno-agriculturists. Such a congregation may also imagine new ways to resist the gods of profit and productivity and enact their own vision of agriculture, which reflects respect for the earth, the town, the family, the community. A suburban Toronto congregation threatened by internal divisions and conflict may be a beachhead of forgiveness and reconciliation by mutually confessing their sins and planning specific acts of reconciliation and renewal.

Salvation in the here and now includes these, and many other, beachheads of the reign of God. "See how they love one another," the world will say, if the Christian community, in its life of worship

---

4 Christiaan Beker, *Paul the Apostle* (Philadelphia: Fortress Press, 1980), 155.

of God and service to others, takes on the very shape and character of the gospel. The shape and character of the gospel, lived out in the community of believers, is made visible by the fruit of the Spirit, including love, joy, peace, patience, kindness, generosity, faithfulness, gentleness, and self-control, as the list in Galatians 5:22–23 puts it. The gospel of Jesus Christ is seen visibly when the church makes room for others. Not just those like us are the church. As broad and deep as God's love, so the church must welcome the stranger, the foreigner, the different, and the strange.

Another beachhead for the dawning of God's new world in the present tense is Christian worship. Good worship is a profoundly countercultural act. In a world that calculates time by money, Christian worship is a holy waste of time. The community gathers and together praises, petitions, confesses, and goes out to serve. Believers are cleansed in the waters of baptism, fed with the bread and wine of the Lord's Supper, and shaped by the preaching of the Word of God in Scripture. All these acts are quite literally worthless in the ways a consumerist world counts worth.

Sometimes, even Christians forget that worship is a beachhead of the coming reign of God. Even Christians can fall into the cozy assumption that worship ought to make us feel warm and snug. Writer Geddes MacGregor tweaks this familiar tendency by writing a prayer that the coddled and comfortable might pray: "O dear, wonderful Father of our incredibly unbelievable experience, we like to feel assured that we may always come to thee when we feel like it. . . . And now, dear Lord, we want quite naturally and simply and just in a word to ask thee very frankly, to give us our heart's desire. Thou art the Comforter, as the old story puts it, and so thou art our friend, for we are very fond of comfort."[5]

When Christians worship, they do so to give glory to God. They do so to identify themselves as followers of Jesus. They do so to align themselves with the purposes of God both now and in the future. They do so in their hymns of praise and in their cries of

---

[5] Geddes MacGregor, *From a Christian Ghetto* (London: Longmans, Green & Co., Ltd., 1954), 93, quoted in Roland M. Frye, *Perspective on Man: Literature and the Christian Tradition* (Philadelphia: Westminster Press, 1961), 149.

lament. Excellent worship is a small glimpse of the reign of God launched in Jesus Christ and coming in all its fullness in God's own good time.

Writer Steven Vryhof tells the story of a glimpse of God in worship.

One Sunday morning, years ago, I entered a Lutheran church in a small village on the coast of Sweden. Perhaps because of the early hour, or the lure of a beautiful summer morning, or the effects of state-run Lutheranism, there were only fourteen congregants gathered. The minister was a slender, blonde lad who had to be fresh out of seminary. I struggled with the Swedish hymns and the Lutheran tendency to stand to pray and sit to sing, the opposite of what I was used to. I joined the others at the front railing for communion, taking the bread and the wine, then returning to my seat.

While the minister, his back to us, was putting away the elements, a parishioner, a middle-aged woman, returned to the front, this time pushing an old woman, presumably her mother, in a wheelchair. The mother had the classic nursing-home look: slumped to the right, thin, scraggly, colorless hair, vacant eyes, and a slack-jaw with her tongue showing a bit. She was here for communion. There was an awkward minute as we all waited for the minister to notice the two waiting at the railing. He finally did turn, perceived the situation, and proceeded to retrieve the elements. He carefully administered the bite of bread and the sip of wine to the old woman. And then he paused, and I held my breath, because I knew what was going to happen next. The young minister looked at the old woman, physically a *wreck* of a human being, and he said to her the most important words that one human being can say to another human being. The minister looked her right straight in the eye and he said to her, "Vår Herre Jesus Krist, vem kroop och blod ni har tatt emot, bevara din själ til evigh liv." *Our Lord Jesus Christ, whose body and blood you have received, preserve your soul unto everlasting life.*

And I suppose it was a coincidence, but it was a God-given coincidence nonetheless. At that precise moment, the bells of the church started pealing, ringing and resonating and resounding and reverberating through the church and through me, making the hair on the back of my head stand up. Heaven touched

earth and it seemed that Vår Herre Jesus Krist, himself was saying, "Yes! I *will* do that!" And then the Father and the Spirit
joined the Son, and using the same words given to Julian of Nor-
wich, the Triune God proclaimed loudly over the ringing of the
bells, "I *may* make all things well, and I *can* make all things
well, and I *shall* make all things well, and I *will* make all things
well; and you will see yourself that *every kind of thing will be
well!*"[6]

In a final sense, Jesus Christ saves us for all eternity, when every
tear will be wiped away and peace and harmony will be restored
to creation. The book of Revelation, in chapter 21, describes this
restoration as a new heaven and a new earth. It is described as a
place of peace and joy, of beauty and abundance. It is not the bor-
ing, misty place some people imagine, perhaps from Sunday
school teachers who sweetly declared that in heaven we would
sing praises to God all day, every day, forever. Children do not see
an eternity like this as particularly inviting. These children grow
up to become adults who do not see an eternity like this as particularly inviting either.

The exact blueprint of heaven is known to no one. Perhaps we
can learn to speak Japanese and to play the cello in heaven. Maybe
we can finally play tennis really well and read all the great clas-
sics. Maybe we will be able to identity all flora and fauna by their
Latin names or climb the ten highest mountain peaks. Such imag-
inative leaps sometimes occupy the thoughts of Christians in their
idlest moments. Such thoughts are not frivolous, however. It is
good for believers to dream and imagine and wonder what is in
store for us when God puts all things right. But, for now, it is
enough to know that the new heaven and the new earth will be a
place of safety and nourishment, a place where all the nations of
the earth will join in harmony with one another and praise to God.
The hope of such a future with God calls the church to live in the
light of that new community now, looking for glimpses of God's
future in the most ordinary events of the present.

---

[6] Steven Vryhof, "Crash Helmets and Church Bells," *Perspectives,* August/September
2000, 3. Used by permission.

The baptism liturgy of the church I attend contains a truly astonishing and powerful moment. The minister, remarkably, addresses the baby just before the baptism itself. The minister holds the baby, looks right at her, and says, "Rachel, it was for you that Jesus Christ came into the world; for you he died and for you he conquered death; yes, for you, little one, you who know nothing of it as yet. We love because God first loved us." It is as dramatic a moment of Christian worship as I have ever seen. This new little person is being introduced to the great claims of the Christian faith. She, too, will learn of the love of God in Jesus Christ, who was born, lived, died, and rose again, for us and for our salvation.

John 3:16, surely the most famous verse of the Bible, says, "For God so loved the world that he gave his only Son, so that everyone who believes in him may not perish but may have eternal life." This is the full truth of the gospel. Perhaps the power and beauty of this verse have been obscured by posters or banners at televised football games with "John 3:16" scrawled on them. Perhaps its familiarity blunts the remarkably good news it proclaims. Perhaps seeing this verse on faded billboards in quaint King James English gives the impression of a quaint, old-fashioned religion. The very next verse, as if to anticipate our wandering interest, insists yet again, "Indeed, God did not send the Son into the world to condemn the world, but in order that the world might be saved through him." To this, the whole church of Jesus Christ throughout the centuries since his ascension shouts, sighs, or weeps, "Alleluia. Amen!"

The Nicene Creed

We believe in one God,
 the Father, the Almighty, maker of heaven and earth,
 of all that is,
  seen and unseen.

We believe in one Lord, Jesus Christ,
 the only Son of God,
 eternally begotten of the Father,
 God from God, Light from Light,
 true God from true God,
 begotten, not made,
 of one Being with the Father;
 through him all things were made.
 For us and for our salvation
  he came down from heaven,
  was incarnate of the Holy Spirit and the Virgin Mary
  and became truly human.
  For our sake he was crucified under Pontius Pilate;
  he suffered death and was buried.
  On the third day he rose again
  in accordance with the Scriptures;
  he ascended into heaven
  and is seated at the right hand of the Father.
  He will come again in glory to judge the living and the dead,
  and his kingdom will have no end.

We believe in the Holy Spirit, the Lord, the giver of life,
 who proceeds from the Father and the Son,
 who with the Father and the Son is worshiped and glorified,

who has spoken through the prophets.
We believe in one holy catholic and apostolic Church.
We acknowledge one baptism for the forgiveness of sins.
We look for the resurrection of the dead,
and the life of the world to come. Amen.[1]

---

[1] *The Constitution of the Presbyterian Church (U.S.A.),* Part I, *Book of Confessions* (Louisville, Ky.: Office of the General Assembly, Presbyterian Church (U.S.A.), 1999), 1.1–.3.